th influenza
uv logik

bill bissett

talonbooks   **vancouver**   **1995**

copeerite © 1995 bill bissett

publisht with th assistans uv th c a n a d a   c o u n c i l

Talonbooks
201-1019 east Cordova
Vancouver British Columbia
Canada V6A IM8

typset in librarian n printd n bound in canada by hignell printing ltd.

1st printing: august 1995

eye want 2 thank th canada council 4 arts award 2 me
n also gratefulee thank th ontario arts council

sum uv thees pomes apeerd previouslee in *all my pomes ar abt yu*
[st paul minnesota] bomb threat check list [minneapolis minnesota]
rampike [toronto] *th ordr uv things* [toronto] *imagine* [st paul]
contemporaree authors autobiographee serees vol 19 gale reserch [detroit]
tongue tide [vancouvr bc]

thanks 2 ben kennedy 4 building th compewtr desk sew great n
4 smudging th apartment n 2 richard browning 4 helping me sew
lerning th compewtr n 2 carol malyon xcellent time sharing prson
n 2 don richardsons compewtr class at see school etobicoke
thanks 2 margaret avison 4 permisyun 2 use her lines from "snow" in
"th throbbing moon" n 2 darien n sharon from whos colleksyun
my drawing apeers on p 3 n 2 george n jeanne johnston from whos
colleksyun my drawing apeers on p 4

front n back covr photographee by allan rosen

ths book is 4 paul duguay

Canadian Cataloguing in Publication Data

bissett, bill, 1939-
    th influenza uv logik

    Poems.
    ISBN 0-88922-357-2

    I. Title.
    PS8503.I88I5   1995   C811'.54   C95-910326-0
    PR9199.3.B5415   1995

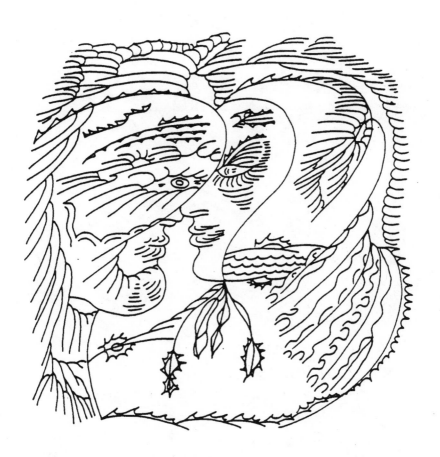

will jim bakker start up

his ministree agen in jail will he get mor chocolate
n vaseleen than aneewun els always an ovr acheevr th
laydee next 2 me on th plane is telling me her son in
law just died no warning heart attack   onlee 44 n
her husband died 2 yeers ago alzheimers

iuv bin sitting heer worreed abt my love life how iuv
got 2 take it eezee or get it luckee i hold her hands
trying 2 comfort her its all so skaree sumtimes   what
duz ths tell me abt love n working n life thn i dont
beleev what th laydee goez on 2 tell me bcoz thers a
deth in her familee sheul get half her fare reimbursd

whn air canada told her that she sd she was compleetlee
thrilld ium thinking if air canada wer 2 tell me that
iud onlee b parshulee thrilld i hold her n say i hope
things get bettr 4 her soon   she nods off n i go in 2
th gallee talk with th stewards if they have th time

wun steward tells me her husband is a pilot n has just
flown back from saudi arabia ths was a yeer bfor th gulf
war   n he told her that locusts ovr a foot long each
have enterd saudi arabia   peopul trying 2 get suppr
redee   o thees damn locusts so far theyr onlee a foot
long

n huge insects she addid with 32 stingrs ar wasting
peopul totalee in india   why 32 stingrs wudint wun
dedlee stingr b enuff   natur dusint take anee chances

sew i answerd an ad   n he arrivd   mistr sumtimes

xcellent we did lots uv stuff 2gethr had 3 or 4 dates
eye think it was on th 5th date he pourd beer ovr us whil
we wer cumming i had dun lots uv nu things with him it
was veree cold outside n he was interesting   he thot i was
cool but sins i dont drink effekts uv a brain op previous
time zone had alredee told him ths it was 2 much uv   a
stretch 4 me still i soldyeerd on it was th kind uv nite as
long as no wun is getting hurt yu try 2 go with th possibul
xperiens in case it can leed 2 sum intimasee sum joint
ventur sum wayze out uv th always encroaching formalisms
fine with out it uv cours yet sew raging n xcellent if it can
take place   like retraysing my steps in a forest that has al
redee changd th influenza uv logik

fine he sz hes confusd lies down on th bed sz he mite
stay fine i sd looking at th green candul uv th nude male
with th hed burnd off now th shouldrs ar going n ium
working on th long pome *th royal unkul n th nite callr
mistr turquois* its a strong nite n thn he sits up n sz
iuv gotta go fine i sd always accepting thn he collapses

backward onto th bed saying i think iul stay thats fine i
sd is ths a veree common human situaysyun a painting
ium working on catches my eye walk him 2 th elevator
he apologizes sz hes a mess i say i think yr wundrful
thats my mistake ther i gave 2 much reassurans 2 b
interesting if i want 2 see him agen   its gonna b a veree
long n live thru it nite wun uv thos veree gud 4 lyrik
meditativ pomes ium thinking ths as well   fine yes

as i walk back in 2 th painting   wet brush in hand

rabid   racoons

what is that in th bushes whn yr   tryin 2 b
so cool   goin 4 a midnite stroll   why its a
rabid racoon

what is that in th chimnee cummin down 2
fast thers no fire on   n whn did yu evr
get it kleend   its a rabid racoon

whos that cummin ovr 2 shake yr hand   in th dark
           like a politishan   its a rabid racoon

whats that undr yr bed   whn yu thot yu wer
sleepin alone   2 bad so sad   its a rabid racoon

rabid racoons ar evreewher we ar askd not 2
approach them   on anee basis theyr cummin up 4 air
from nu york hitchin rides on th undrside uv great
transports spredding thru ontario   toronto soon sew
infestid   reports ar suggestid   th media sz

th racoons striped tuxedos   doncha touch muukus
   formrlee sew fetching   dripping from theyr eye balls
      now frozn saliva   o doncha touch

whos that answrin yr door 4 yu whn yr cumming
home   whn ther was no wun ther   whn yu   left

mistr n missus rabid   racoon

runnin yr bath 4 yu   scrambling sum eggs 4 u biting
yu   4 sum antee pasto   n throwin yu ovr th balkonee
   unkul pasto   th weight liftr

why   its th rabid racoons   th rabid racoons   yes

dansing with my skin 4 partee hats

7

instant   evreething

givn that yuv got enuff food in th
fridg   smoke   if yu dew   th rent is paid nowun
is terriblee mad at yu   n yu feel sumhow
yu ar taking care uv yrself   sum what   yuv
gottn layd a coupul times ths past week at
leest   if yu wantid   or needid   n shared great
companee in conversaysyun   n yr health is ok
hey its all fr now   isint evreething alredee heer
n a dash uv free will   well into th dna
puppetree receipe not mor thn a dash
uv free will is required   we dont want 2 much
uv it   fine   n th building is not on fire   go
eezee on th coffee   n have a hot bath inbetween
work play cyculs mor abstrakt nouns based on th
theereez uv opposits binaree nosyuns ther   evreething
is mor than that   ium having multi lateral talks
with my self he sd   she sd xcellent   th snow is
totalee falling   falling ovr ths orange coastal
citee

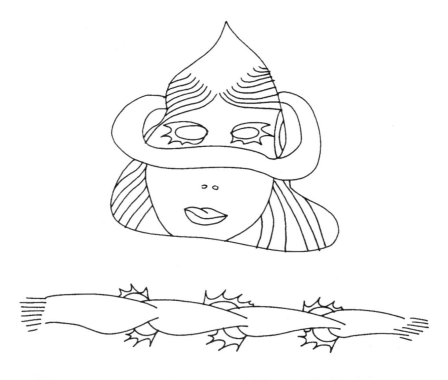

LOVE IS TH DREEM N TH DANSE NEVR ENDS N WHO CAN FORGET

love is th dreem n th danse nevr ends n who can forget   love is th dr
eem n th danse nevr ends n who can forget   love is th dreem n th
danse nevr ends n who can forget love is th dreem n th danse nevr
ends n who can forget   love is th dreem n th danse nevr ends n who
can forget   ======oo====oooo====oooo====oooo====ooo===oo==
==========ooooooo====oooo====oooo=====oooo====oooo=====
ridin with jimmee so far   riding with jimmee o wow ====ooo=====
ridin with jimmee so far   riding with jimmee o wow =====ooo====
 ==========oooooooo=======oooooooo=======ooooooo======
==========oooooooooooo======ooooooooo======oooooooo==
ther ar no bugs at ths altitude   n th wind sweeping thru   ther ar no
bugs at ths altitude n th wind sweeping thruuuuuuuuuuuooo===ooo
oooooooooooo=========ooooooooooooo========oooooo====
============ooooooooo========ooooooooooo======ooooooo==
=========oooooooo=====ooooooooooooo=========oooooo====
its all merging with th spirit ridrs   sailing with th fire   merging with th
spirit ridrs sailing with th fire ridrs sailing with th fire with th fire===
=========oooooooo========oooooooooo========ooooo======
=======oooooo======oooooooo======oooooo====ooo===ooooooo
our poneez go so fast   purpul mountains ice peeks   thers no tests an
ee mor 2 hold us no games aneemor 2 scold us we go out uv th town
out uv th hills   byond th roads=============oooooooo=====ooooo
=========oooooooo========ooooooo=======oooooo====ooo
==========oooooooo========oooooo=========oooooo====ooo
whats it 2 yu whats it 2 ya wer goin so fast   whats it 2 us whats it 2
us evreething whethr it lasts   we go from heer riding from heer jimm
ee n me   jimmee n me==========oooooooo========ooooo===ooo
==========oooooooooo=========oooooooo=======oooooo===
eezee on th plannin past ths moment share th food share th joy eez
ee on eezee on cudduling in th sleepin blankit   undr th stars   trust
in th unseen enerjeez our leedrs can nevr tell us abt=========ooo==
================ooooooooooo=========ooooooooo=====oo
==========oooooooooo===========ooooooooooo========ooo
ridin with jimmee so far   ridin with jimmee o woww   ridin with jimm
ee o woww   ridin with jimmee so far riding with jimmee o wowwww==
=============ooooooo========ooooooooo=======ooooo=====
===========oooooo========oooooooooo=======ooooo=======
love is th dreem n th danse nevr ends n who can forget ooo====oooo

th umbrella uv is allan gardns   rising

snow is always filling my eyez sumtimes its
veree beautiful   th prson who set fire 2 th
building is back in   in her same apartment
alredee renovatid   yelling veree amazing
i nevr gave her matches cigarets yes thers
talking in th lobbee whatevr i dont think
sheul try it agen   ium mooving out aneeway
thers almost no time 2 get usd 2 things

getting usd 2 things is that impliez meens
sayz resonates raging can b goin 2 sleep
now   sew manee frends goin 2 spirit   sumtimes
ium crying   sumtimes ium angree   thers a lot
uv sumtimes   sereen   numb staring at th green
hous baking with snow   graceful curvs uv its
glass shimmring roof   sky line   lites dotting
th raven air   snow n cold evreewher   its nite
etsetera   atmospheer uv promises n   what is

me n my monkeez wer laffing 2nite xcellent
eye heer chimes they ar beautiful as ths nite
sew glacial stillness slite wind mooving th
chimes in th frozn air   like radiating from
off th blu snow   th animals uv our minds run
skittring ovr th ice   wher th fountains will
b agen in th summr not eezee   yet 2 dreem
uv that cumming   see flowrs   all around me
growing surging apeering   whil a frend is
disapeering from ths world thees flowrs
humidify   worlds n construkts colliding
n in sew manee parallell wayze   continuing
evreewher

th animals go 2 sleep not far from th mush
room ship maypul leef gardns   memoreez uv
ancient rhythms breething warm cup my hands
our freezing bones soup uv th futur fieree
furnace   humming birds fly from reliving th
lafftr   reliving th lines   looking 4

ther was an evil prime minister

who sold out his countree 2 th neighbouring
empire   we lernd gradualee 2 not care
caring can leed 2 stress

so we workd like crayzee n drempt like gold
n got thru ths hard time told each othr our
storeez n uv our love   n sigh

startid agen

th chemikul man from trois rivières

is not reelee from trois rivières ths is a trew storee eye
dont want 2 get sued not 2 far from ther tho   well he
sd with free trade its terrifik our c e o s in mexico
citee wher theyul stay at leest 4 a whil ern 3o,ooo cdn
pr yeer ther they can live like royaltee on that wheras
in trois rivières it was costing 15o,ooo pr annum pr
uv cours we always have a nashunalist on th bord gud
4 p r yu gotta make sure they always can b outvotid
arrange things 4 that by phone whatevr with th othr
membrs way bfor th ackshul meeting   uv cours i sd

also great he sd putting his hand on my leg n giving
it an introducktoree squeez is ther ar no pollushyun
controls in mexico citee so ths is all great dividends
great 4 th stock holdrs i askd o yes he sd th profits
ar way bettr now wasint it veree xpensiv mooving th
plant i askd well no he sd we did receev a subsidee
from th feds 2 help with that ahh i sd that wud help
its a long way from trois rivières 2 mexico citee

as long as th toreez stay in weul b most xcellent he
sd great 4 bizness what if th mexican workrs form
yuunyuns n want bettr pay bettr working condishyuns
i askd lifting firmlee his hand off my leg n puttin it
back on his

i askd ths non judgmentalee what wud he dew thn n
he sd lurching 4ward well we wud just moov   farthr
south or wherevr wher peopul wud b glad 2 work 4
5 dollrs a day   o thats most releeving i sd i hope
as well sins yu will always b lokatid sumwher els yu
wudint reelee pay canadian taxes he lookd at me all
smiles n sd well ther is a lot uv travelling now taxes
ar uv cours less   travelling as yu know can b tiring
veree   but as long as i get home 2 trois rivières week

ends oftn 2 b with th familee iul b okay ths is a big
adjustment espeshulee 4 th canadian workrs i sd yes
he sd staring at me n smiling yuv got it but thers no
thing like familee valus thats th bed rock uv evreething
yes i sd th bed can b rockee fr sure he looks at me that
weird appraising gayze thn deciding like i dew know sum
thing he continuez as long as votrs get a littul mor so
phistikatid stop obsessing abt who aneewun is sleeping
with reelee i sd i meen he sd ium on th road so much
i have 2 get screwd sumtimes as long as i get home 4
my familee on th weekends yes i sd thers a goal ther

n thees profits ar incredibul now he sd yuunyuns wer
asking 2 much theyr hi wages wer adverslee affekting
our profits aneeway soon we ar mooving th chemikuls
from langlee in bc i wundr how they got ther nevr
mind 2 mexico citee th rest uv them boy thos chem
ikuls get around i sd he looks at me smiles sz we dew
have th opn trucks 2 drive th vats vats i askd 2 mexico
citee he sz from langlee bc yes i know thats in bc i sd
he is on a roll now n continuez ths epik narrativ sz
bcoz uv th f t a thers no annoying restriksyuns bcoz
uv th destinaysyun i askd yes he sd yu lern veree fast
thank yu eye sd its neet 2 fly executiv fr a change n

find out abt reelee great things that ar going on yu can
not find thees things out in ekonomee no he sd agree
ing well its onlee coupul hundrid mor he sd is it reel
ee i askd i wundr why mor peopul dont dew that

me i was flying exek bcoz uv frequent flyrpoints reward
sew it was free 2 me it is way mor roomee n we did
have filet mignon its onlee a few hundrid mor if yu
have th exek bookd at leest two weeks in advans n wer
2 say have yr ekonomee bookd at th last minit thats
his frame uv ref othrwize th diffrens is abt tripul a
shame 2 b sew crampd in ekonomee he sd yu can
hardlee breeth in mexico citee but south uv ther wher

we may b abul 2 have our white collar base   say in
kuernavaka its reelee beautiful ther thees ar amazing
times he sd 2 me   if th liberals wer 2 get in now they
cudint change it if they wantid 2   its 2 late

amazing time 2 stay awake yes i sd i herd on a bc ferree
recentlee that dabatts agen i dont wanna get sued has
a bottuling plant in a veree remote part uv china   wher
its almost slave labor uv cours th price domestikalee
is not lowerd wun cent no that may have 2 b inkreesd
bcoz uv th continuing recessyun i askd uv cours he sd
we have 2 keep th dollr up uv cours i sd he sd 2 me yu
lern reelee fast well i sd ium trying 2 pay attensyun n
stay awake   its worth it isint it yes indeed he sd   all
wayze

atavism

```
ata  via  tiva  miva      sima  vita
ata  visa  iva  misa  sivati  vati
ita  vasi  viva  mivat   sita   viti
ata   visa  viva  mivati  sivati simmmmmm
ati  viavam  vima mivatma  simmmmmm
tia  ismavata  misa  meesa    sitamvati
tia  ismivatavati    misata  mista  aitamvateee
iata ismitavi  ata  mistava  sitamvati  eevatee
sita  m  n  m    is    sitam    seeta    vima
  n   mmmmm  nnnnnn isa seeta seetavi veema
vatam ata istannnn  iiiii  isatmavi sta tava ata
istavat  istavatam  ava va  ava vi  sava  tava  ata
vim ata miv siv astam sata via viti vita vii vata
visavatamavata ti visatavatamati mi tasvamisa via
 si ni tiv ni tasvamisa mi tasvamisa via tiasvaatam
avats amavata visavat ti ama sata astam asta at v
istana istama istava istata istatiii vastiii vista tiii
  am  sit am  vit  am  viitii  amsitvit  ma tiv  am vit
eeeee tiva teeva tavi tima amsee  timmmmmmmm
is via viti tiva teeva tavi tima amsee  timmmmmm
aaa teema sativm atisa vmmmmmm satis ativa smmm
tiva is vit a si tivim tivin vina visa vita  vama vana
vannnnnnnnnsativa  tavis  tamis  tanim  tisva vammm
vammmmmm  ateesa  vmmmm  istamvi  tisa vam siti
vvvvv  immmmmmm  ammmmm  ateeva  smmm  stava
istameee tisa van tisavinam vas as va veesa ta teeza
tia sati tiva tava tima tina taa visa vam vat vit vis
a vee siv mit mia miv miva mis misa a mita miavam
mista miastavam veesta avi vam aveee va avia asa avi
  avis vias  viat tavi sit  i  va  stam va vastee  iiiiii
       sat vism ata ata asa aia ava ama
         tavi  at   va va va va veeeeee
                 va va va va veeeeeeee
         sa teeeeva   va va va va veeeee
         as  eeeetva   va va va va vaaaaa
```

at last ium faxd in th turning bliss uv th tidal town

sixteen wun n six make sevn   sevn tides   a ring

uv sevn glaciers   sevn beets 2 th bar   in ths pattern

sevn times sevn is
                        its all abt confidens abt being
sevn times summr tides   touching gliding so eezee
n cool into th allee n th backyard off th street n
                              its all abt
dewin it   touching turning glands n all th mur
muring heart   spreding in 2   emerald lakes
                              emerald dreems
sevn outside th   th town   wun n six
    emerald rice   villages   make sevn
          fields   farms   emerald suns
                                     emerald moons
  wun n six   dairee   gonna go
feeding   2 rubee silvr
          sew
make sevn   mouths   telling   hevn   swallowing
    yes n air   breth   blood   rushing
    make sevn   medow   green emeralds uv
dripping mirage   living   lotus   wheet

    sevn mouths   savd by th at last ar fanning   out
    from my wun mouth breething   skin smell   yu

    n ium home fr a whil   n its thank yu   n no

thank yu yes   thank yu n it sure is great n th
    moon   i see it up ther is full n ium so   full
                              its all abt
    n eezee   like it was always gonn a last   ths time
              like it was always gonna last ths time
              like it was always gon   last ths time

life can have difficult moments

evn in th rekreaysyunal area uv th geriatrik ward we wer
visiting in big hospital things wer fine tho not festiv
a lot uv eldrlee peopul sitting pissing zoneing on sum
propaganda on tv th nurses at th staysyun bgan verbalee
abusing a patient saying reelee meen things 2 her me n my
frend bcame concernd stoppd talking among ourselvs our
frend we wer visiting was passing out agen eye went ovr 2 th
patient th three women nurses who had bin verbalee abusing
her saying shut up til we get time why ar yu all wayze whin
ing shut up we dont care they hadint realizd we wer ther
from theyr staysyun wher they wer sitting dewing not much
taking a brek they cudint see us pillar in btween th nurses
lookd shockd angree as i tendrlee touchd th eldr patient
on her shouldrs n askd her what wud yu like

wun nurs got it 2gethr came ovr 2 help th patient she b
came reelee sweet tho upset they had bin observd th patient
was being upset abt th straps being 2 tite holding her in 2
her chair they wer hurting her wrists th nurs had bcum
caring tord th patient aftr verbalee abusing her shes sorree
now th othr nurses still cast angree thretening glances at
me i had intrveend they slowlee realize they had bin ob
servd n had bettr change mode they look resentful abt ths

th nurs who bcame nice wer all human if givn a chance that
is can change 4 th bettr was finding a mor comfortabul
chair 4 ths patient she was fragile curlee thin wispee white
hair her eyez pleeding entreeting 4 sum kindness sum
speshul regard th nice nurs was loosning th straps ths
eldr had probablee givn birth known youthful passyuns
smelt strawbereez evreewher had bin evreewher thees nurses
wud b going she gets 2 b in th geriatrik ward being yelld at
by three othr women in uniform ths is a possibul fate 4
manee whatevr gendr whatevr th staysyun isint it it is
shocking tho isint it

i went back 2 my frends wun she sd that was a terribul
abuse uv powr ium glad yu intrveend certainlee she addid
abuse uv powr is not relatid 2 gendr tho th medikul praktise
is a male dominatid industree she addid with what i knew
2 b an ironik comment   it was anothr difficult moment

19

th prins in th palace

is standing on th balkonee looking out ovr th magik
pools n th rising gardns summring lush up from th
    loamee n so verdant vallee reflekting in th eclipsing
    lite th resident watrs n th loving gardeners hands
around each othr gracefulee stumbuling 2 th erths floor
    wer it 4 mangos or peaches in each othrs mouths they
    kiss n embrayse into wizardlee witchlee   sand

th prins sz i know ium onlee fulfilling a role i will grow
    out uv narrowing baritone tremors or hopefulee nevr
grow up   ther th lies onlee ar turning into lustrous
blu green being its nevr that always he has seen limbs
torn from theyr axes herd th cries n skreems from th tortur
centr deep in th crokodile nests uv th equalitee palace
        has tourd th cells uv libinaysyuns so frownd on by th
    mor austeer galactik haruumphing heds th prins works on
committeez 2 improov evree thing th qween n king have
    told him ths takes time like turning 2 gold duz as we all
dew moist clouds sighing filld with th veins uv so manee
    lovrs sumtimes beckoning entreeting going on thru th
    cloud countreez wher angels ar holding th erth up whil
    sew sensualee languidlee making love with each othr in
finitlee n rushing within so far secret 2 us heer dimensyuns
wher paths uv stars make wayze thru th thundring brekrs
    uv sounds n hedlong comets hurling stone showr
                                        melodeez

    wun day his monkeez wer lost from him 4 a whil n that
    taut him a lot abt what all peopul go thru as if he didint
    alredee know troubuling with attachments sew inevitabul
        is it 2 far is it 2 neer ar we afrayd uv closeness will we
    get hurt abandond agen is that it letting go uv insecuriteez
    feers oftn so full uv sorrows n so full uv magik   oftn th
    less we try 2 undrstand or whn th state is benign n reelee

20

includes evree wun thatul b th day we can heer agen what
th othr animals ar saying 2 us
is that WHN   theyr dansing n leep
ing in th crystal watrs th hopi philosophers
say th time we will all undrstand each othr   will
cum agen n rubee sparkling zirkonia n soddn straw he
wud lay on with his visitors in th barn his lips btween
theyr cheeks uv   theyr eyez   n all th whil th musik
playing drums flute blu birds flying

out uv th bay tamboreens mandolin he thinks
sumday he wunt b prins will he b king   iuv oftn
royalee fuckd up he sighd tho by whos standards n what
abt th compassyun barometr   who dusint get confusd   burn
themselvs   oftn iuv bin reelee 2gethr what diffrens so manee
contra dicktoree construkts floating around fine evreewuns
view sew diffrent not leening hard on th railing wind raging
in his hair   his eyez sailing in 2 th forevr dahlia gardenias
tunas orkeeda dansing frolicking with th qween n king uv th
taybul watrs   dolphin frendlee   rapturous in theyr lolling
sew fine i know god has manee names n is un nameabul he
muses n certainlee wun uv gods names is our selvs reelee cud
ths b wun uv my happee n sereen moments in my life 4 me
at ths time looking out at th green n radiant unfolding vista
is ther a line up 4 our dreems 2 get 2 th veree possibul grace
uv th singul life touching hearts genitals   flowrs dreems
whats reel passing thru tapestreez in th flying sand will all
th apparentlee nevr 2 b xplaind reelee losses   n kisses

n methoda uv klass n hierarkeez go thru changing breething
so that evree wun is let in   he gazes at th 2 gardeners
each in th othrs embrayse   his 2 his at last

finding th watr   uv spirit n continuez breething whil
th pink rose tree   next 2 him   on th balkonee is singing

uv yu   n uv all th growing stretching n th sew   enchanting

nite uv ths storee tellrs blu jade   dreeming

**jet lag n kulshur shock aftr arriving back in th
coastal area   aftr almost 6 months in centralia**

its way bettr thn being coverd with spidr
webs   as engrossing as that mite b wudint it
  evenshulee b choking n wher thers a vast n intrikate
network uv webbing   wudint ther b spidrs small wuns
delikate ballereena style leggings big hairee wuns
  coupul bites n theyve got me th inside tendrills uv
spidrs can b veree wiree ripping us apart as they gorge
us down   thees ar th veree large spidrs mottuld
    speckuld chimnee soot gleemee   with a suddn

  fanfare uv deth around theyr eyez   watching us 4 a
whil until they lazeelee make theyr moov   ther ar

  th othr spidrs   uv cours much smallr   who entr us thru
all our orifices   cumming at us   from th showr   up at us
  from th toilet   they like us 2 b not thnking uv them   pry
opn our eyelids go in ther   hacking into th pupil   or undr
th fingr n toe nails

  thees efforts belie th fact uv manee benign spidrs
who want onlee 2 sing 4 us sing us 2 sleep in our futons
   postyr pedik   whatevrs til wer all totalee safe n sound
in eternitee trusting in th whol process that is nevr
  ending by definishyun n oftn interesting   thees

  ar th spidrs we pray 2 build ikons 2   oftn draped in
gossamer   gesturs uv blessings tord us   spidr teers
   dropping from theyr manee eyez   4 all our suffring

thees ar th lap spidrs   i was feeling sew alienatid
   ths nite huge non benign spidr faces looking in my
sunset beech window   wher not far away i cud see english
bay th infinit blu silvr gold turquois crimson vista uv
   th pacifik sky air   leeding me out eye escaped

went walking deliberatlee casualee hands in pockits
trying 2 b trusting whn ther is such terror uv judgment
n just plain attack in ths world its skaree 2 say

  nothing uv th continuing thret uv th huge spidrs othr
peopul can b enuff problema   n breething th see air
    moistur getting usd 2 it now aftr a long abeyans
  n still psychikalee veree unstedee   spidr notes wer in
th air   hanging from buildings

          n he saw me   a frend   we totalee huggd   angel
sew great   ium feeling bettr   n we raged on   destina
  etsetera veree cool n eye felt strongr   walking ths
  walk is working   met sum othr angel   she hugging me
    ar yu well yes take care   love yu so great   n i went
on we wer blowing kisses sew wundrful n

eye went SHOPPING got xcellent food tuk it home
xcellent   great went 2 sleep agen fr a whil   during
  evreething feeling alpha suspending thinking feeling
    how great   ther ar
                          angels who love me us EVREE
WHER
            they wll always find us if we get just a littul
courageous evn if we dont n hug us n love us n we feel

    th angel   embrayse th tendr care always sew neer

ps th second angel she sd call me ium in
    th book i lookd n lookd n cudint find
    eye think shes in th angel book   anothr
    way uv finding n

its th circuls our minds get stuk in   evn offring
our throats

                linking obsessiv thots 2 crankee focus whos
          looking 4 ultimate or evn periferal teeth meening 2
     base our lives on mouth 2
                                   circuls   that choke us
     handul us so gruff poor us undun in2 submissyun
        heers a surrogate ths a facsimile that so reminding uv
     what propels us 2 feel wer not all heer
                                        what takes th
          living from us keeps us 2 dimensyunal hers his rule
     thsul dew iul just follow that n evreething will b fine
         stuk in fine she dusint have it he dusint have it
     onlee it has it fine okay
                                  it had raind all week wheras
          letting go uv th circuls theyr so fiers sumtimes   they
     hurt us   we go out into our   lives salmon running
        close ovr our dreems alredee ar sun neck spine
     bones fingr eyez   green salel   red berreez what is ar
     we want 2 define our self selvs whn   its so elastik fluid
        three baloons wer flying above   us   i opend th creem
     cannister was pouring coffee spreding taybul cloths
          touching each othrs feet undr aftr gettin it on with yu
     i dont want 2 cruis no mor   will ths pass

            joy phond in leeving   eye remembr th x

        th message   uv c o ur s   plosyun as if it wer
           we walk on sand   ystrday tongue feet th
           all   wayze   gold thundr sky goin off
                                        like fire works
                                      lightning in th hall
          we wer all left with throbbing hed aches as if sum
        thing legs arms strange feeling in th joints swimm
     ing longnesses as if sumthing had rippd our throats
        out   leeving a mark on our minds   wer they

th vessul

was so awkwardlee construktid
manee joints not reelee meeting   or dovetailing n
th xcessiv amounts uv nails reelee rusting
n sum parts uv th sails shredding   that it was see
worthee mor from wishing thn from effikayshus building

indeed what wud bcum uv us all on ths wonkee voyage
faith 2 moov oceans   courage 2 calm n dispell giant waves

imaginaysyun 2 not faltr altho well restid during dreeree
desulatoree dayze n nites   without wind or moon or stars
evn if they ar long sins gone from our possibul
present site   give romantik lite   n pre scientifik
inspiraysyuns 2 our fingrings uv th nodulaysyuns uv deus
x destina wher els wud we b going toward   or inside

uv cours ther ar always moments uv sexual reegret n
thees ar oftn misaprehensyuns uv th most baroque ordring
whn all is wanting that is wanting   is wanting n care
being part uv th dansing

well heer uv cours ther is also scrubbing th decks n   nu
identiteez cropping up supplanting   eye dont think sew
can   aneewun   replaysing eithr   not 2 evn think uv
adding mor n mor peopul   fresh   xciting 2 turn from
it is 2 leen on th past problema   not let go uv th
satisfying n unsatisfying parenting   take our own
journee   veree few xcuses 2 ourself is wher it is
counting   reelee   4 not going on

precawsyun   uv cours always   yet if th bell is ringing
dew try n answr it   howevr gracefulee   if at all possibul
wudint yu rathr b loving   well thers a pawsing   in th
puritan withdrawl from adventur   n plesur th bodee is
reelee as fine as aneething   is connekting with th
mind
n guilt from societal teechings freys th

delikate
n potenshulee strong n yielding n being asking
among th treez   furthr in th summree blowee
winds n breezes yu can feel on yr skin   making
agen th innosent music we can live 4

wun uv my ship mates had a small gold statue uv
a barracuda sumtimez he sd it was a salamandr as
well as a trinket also gold uv sum minatur merkats
thees wer all deliteful 2 me n oftn undr a full moon he
wud show thees 2 me on th uppr deck th ship jostuling
its nevrthless way no mattr th emosyuns uv wondr i wud
feel looking at thees objects or it th ship wud seem n
th watr n sky also 2 coinside evn merg with th feelings i
wud b xperiensing at thees times
he wud tell me
manee storeez on thees occasyuns how he had
acquired 2 my mind thees tresurs n wher all he had
been happee n sad n dangrous n himself in dangr
oftn
in my bunk aftr i wud endlesslee repeet 2 my
self evree thing he had relatid 2 me its importans n its
detail he wud sumtimez smile curving his lip into th
uttrmost mystereez that i felt sure nowun els cud undr
stand or evr dreem uv putting into words n i wud fall
asleep agen phrasing n rephrasing n listning 2 his
words n seeing ovr n ovr agen that smile how it did
curv like a magikul gold crescent moon into th dark nite
n th watr
slapping n carressing th serpentine bow as
we made our way thru anothr endless xpans like i hoped
peopuls minds wud b like i sumtimes thot they wer
espeshulee his tho i was alredee starting 2 find limits n
circuls clockwork n chores n feers n th less thn nimbul
sieve th circuitree uv th brain   n ium disapointed at what
seem arbitraree limits in peopul tho not yet in his smile

curving with plesur n unpredicktabul   risk

wun nite he tuk me into his bunk n held me til
dawn whn he left leeving me wun uv his gold
  merkats claspd in my hand   whn i gayzd at it b
for brekfast i saw that it wore his smile as did
my bodee   n my heart

he was no robot

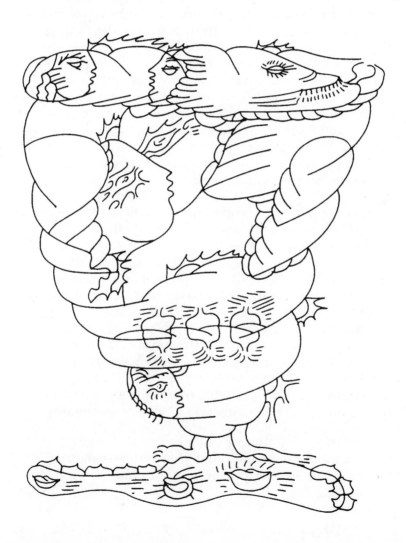

is ther brekfast   or am i hungree

    FIRE   fine ium watching a reelee interesting perry
mason   wun iud nevr seen bfor i didint know who did it
wch was unusual n kept my intrest i was reelee in2 it thn
th alarm   terribul nois i turnd th volume on th tv up hi
evreething continus

during th commershul i notis a lot uv peopul standing in
th courtyard looking up above my apartment its abt 30
below n abt quartr 2 three in th morning th alarms have
bin raging 4 almost half an hour   isint it 2 cold 4 a fire
n evn 2 late   2 erlee 2 interrupting   alarms happn oftn
in ths building sew oftn in fact th alarm system was down
gradid sew it wud take a reelee big blaze 2 set them off   eye
start slowlee   oftn they ar fals alarms putting on my boots
pants swetr jackits etsetera whil goin on watching ths
episode uv perry mason will i nevr know what happns in
ths wun th alarms continu ringing   if yr nois sensitiv at
all wch i am   ths sound is tortur

during th final court scene in ths episode aftr wch anothr
prime suspekt has bin found ded a vois cums out uv th
ceiling wher th alarm has bin skreeching 4 seems like al
most an hour now   n sz   leev th building immediatelee
dress warmlee   stay calm   leev th building immediatelee
stay calm   leev as quiklee as possibul whil being calm it
sz   th fire is on th 7th floor n needs 2 b controlld leev
immediatelee   stay calm i grab my bindr uv most recent
drafts uv pomes ium working on now n in fact leev   not
using th elevators n stay calm whil departing veree
quiklee by taking veree large veree long steps down th
hall n out th door 2 th outside wher th evakuaysyun is
taking place   an engorging scene   places evreewun

iud bin at a partee that nite bfor cumming home wher
ther had bin 4 fire peopul   had that bin was that fire
shadowing   now ther was at leest a hundrid seemd like

28

6-7 big trucks tons n tons uv equipment   whn th
tiny reelee girl woman who we all had bin nice 2 who usd
2 apeer in th lobbee its a 21 storee towr asking 4 cigarets
n sobbing i always gave sumtimes she calld me hunee
was being guidid out th door we wer askd 2 stand back ther
was a wide varietee uv wardrobe sum men wer in lounging
weer sum women wer redee 4 hevee acksyun sum ancient
looking wuns holding theyr parakeets sum lethr guys just
back from theyr clubs totalee lethr we all hudduld intimate
lee 2gethr in big room off th lobbee we had bin allowd in now
xcellent as ovr an hour standing outside in 30 below not great
dressing codes it was a beautiful melange from evreewher all
beleefs all intrpretaysyuns all supporting each othr as they
had strappd th frothee looking girl woman she was weering
pink orange colord pajamas they wer kind 2 her she lookd
numb she had i lernd ther burnd her entire apartment out
n th 12 floors above her wer now smoke inhalatid she had
almost immolatid herself they had kleend her off nicelee
bfor that had happend she had bin coverd with soot as they
bound th last strap tite across her middul she sd loudlee is
ther brekfast or am i hungree we all observd ths politelee
tried 4 warmlee n sum uv us noddid like we know what
yu meen

i askd a fire prson if i cud go back in 2 get my monkeez he sd
no what wud i like my monkeez or my life o i sd sew a lot
uv waiting being asking continuing th buses they sd wer
cumming 4 us   i didint want 2 go on wud yu like 2 wher
wud they b warm take us 2 luxuree hotels

th buses nevr came n just bfor 6 in th morning we wer allowd
back in our apartments xcellent   n i wonderd   wher was
rosee whn went across th street 2 b with her n she didint
seem 2 b ther   dew i spend 2 much time alone   n what can
i dew abt it   is th baybee cumming thru th door   th ideaz
uv wuns own self wuns trew identitee is that merelee wun uv
th infinit or at leest manee ideas WHATS TH BIG IDEA   uv
self wch ar plural n infinitlee dispersing

wud my monkeez n th two yeers uv paintings ium getting redee
4 th kingston show b alrite wud th monkeez look aftr them
had smoke n fire swept my apartment wud ths guy i met in
th lobbee cum back 2 my apartment with me why not if why
not is it part uv th streeming back seremonee 2 discuss evree
thing whatevr was is ther nevr a dull moment starring
irene dunne n fred mcmurray wasint it pay no mind les
wonderd wth all th fire shadowing will we reelee all go up in
smoke sum day howevr starring cheech n chong sd i was
still visiting hotel rooms whn that came out remembr th
laundromat spinning scene

next day that perry mason cums on agen great yet ium sew
tirud from not sleeping during th fire nite i fall asleep agen
just at th nu 2 me part ths is calld frustraysyun will eye
evr know who did it did aneewun was it self infliktid

th fire peopul wer amazing 2 contain that fire uv cours th
prson who startid it didint wish anee uv us anee harm n i
wonderd agen wudint yu is ther brekfast or am i hungree

th big deel

in life he sd   as well as uv cours
accepting n that uv cours can b relaysyunal
suggestid is being responsibul 2 wuns
own desires starting from me wuns self yr
self finding yr own happeeness as long as
yr not hurting aneewun   howevr that is n
shifting   evreething always is event   shulee each mo
ment going 4 it is it a moment its mor molekular mikro
than that   whil also uv cours taking care uv bizness sum
n being abul 2 give 2gethr we all make up th restless
dreem mooving byond yr own feers n needs 2 cling
n watch th fountains flying upward theyr blessing
watrs on yr soul what ar wuns own desires   dont
let aneewun lay guilt or try 2 possess yu or
make yu work 4 them   yu arint responsibul
4 theyr ms mistr guidid confusyuns
taking a long bath   kleering
th labyrintheen cotton wool hard un
abul 2 get around rock faktoree   punching
in n pushing   listning 2 th present   what
theree can xplain it breething being in yr
cardio vascular post swamp modern world listn
ing 2 th messengr in th cruising ground   him saying whn
ar yu going 2 accept yr worreeing abt sum wun upsetting u
whn they cud b dewing totalee fine   accomplishes no
thing skin blood flesh tongue sugar licking
all th flies off th ointment yu suspending in
th shutterd panolpee late summr breez dansing
against th smoke staind curtains yes yu winninglee
wonderd as yr bodee levitating tord th top ceiling uv th
room a round wher th refleksyuns from his eye glasses
as he tickuld yu n tuk them off bfor unbuttoning yr shirt
squeez yr tits so yu sighing bend down ovr undr
him as yu ar eeting n loving his cock n being
n th sun playing in both yr hair his hands
on yr ass rising th plastr shaking
carving embroideree round th
cornrs uv th breething room play

31

attachmentz   xpedishyuns   devosyuns   will ths

fit 4 love 2 th scripts we follo thru we didint write
its not always prsonalee   satisfying   as we lift carree
look up who is rite anothr bomb falling on us making
 sum moov was it reelee blessd by a triad uv diamonds
 hanging in th sky   set in sum gloomee   ultra mareen
 pastyurs set in requitid moments times an orange
 lit return chek in how ar yu brain xchange smiling
 sera bella looping happilee jellee smile mushroom
 dreeming neurologia awake th eyez evn thru th lids
 uv xperiens ar sew touching   seeming 2 smile

looking 4 gold heer th raven calling look 4 silvr in yr
embrace goin down 2 each othr thru all th opnings in 2
 us we can find yr heart speeking 4 love b yr being
 serch 4 help in ths mayze lerning 2 help being with
 th lite sew changing letting in cats shadows climate
 cellular equator cutting th color from yr hair speks
 matching th edging prmitting feeling snow tempra
 tures rising falling pains mirakuls cum creeping
 at agoneez uv frustraysyuns satisfacksyuns accept
 ing letting attempting fresh allowings whil steering
      if can thru th thickning mud curling round us in th
 glow uv th tv rays   living with not running out in
 ice evreewher random falling attaching kathoding at
 taching itselvs 2 th buildings wind tunnuls we beet
   thru echoing skreem
                              asking 4 needid b leeving in
   th journeez uv th marrow being infinit evn if onlee
 now th voyage uv th lamp othr oftn tragik prat falls
 uv th changing moral univers merging with th murkee
see side town rockin in th tap tap tap es treed glimmr
 ing   how dew we trust agen   aftr wev bin hurt loving
 without vulnrabul demons ther ar nun reelee   re
   side   run with them   selvs n th sky

32

wev let them go   keeping opsyuns 4 our
selvs infinit manee folding endlesslee   ther ar no
reel numbrs n ther ar   we moov

on wher th swallows
live housd in th tall sienna clay hills n th eagul fly
ing ovr th sew changing formata uv loving being with
 soaring n ium   landing grabbing on 2   th star fish
 shore making th day   th dramas   possessyuns wch ar
onlee nevr territoreez flowing fluid ekstaseez wher no
   demarkaysyuns occur losing gaining   sleeping
all th self murdrs cellular disintegraysyuns sew
  dormant in th pesticides touching lava grid molek

ular   speeed   transforming serch lites   on   cum in

    shed our clothes on th porch   iuv got 2 eye
    hold yu   agen in time dreem in 2 th   see

    changing evreething

why dew we feer change   feer uv th unknown

can knarl us yet change is all ther is availabul 2 us
it is a mysterious entangulment sumtimes we seem 2 b
stuck with evree thing is going fine tho wev lost out
on a lovd wun   anothr lovd wun is going 2 spirit   2
close that turbulent dipping we hold on 2 life   tho we
know itul go etsetera   we have guides 2 leed us show us
help us   thru sum uv th mor rockee wayze we struggul
off cours 2 accept WHERS TH COURS   WHOS RUNIN
TH SHOW   WE WANT 2 KNOW   yes

we create con
strukts we parshulee or almost compleetlee choos
selekt if we can munee n mobilitee work self valu
acceptans uv our limitaysyuns trying 2 grow thru
letting go uv mooving on desire luck miseree n thos
all cum 2 us

dont cry my frend   its onlee a dreem
dont cry my frend   weul wake up soon n danse 4evr
in th rainbow clouds upliftid

thers a loophole in evree
model we make   they ar all leeking we evn what they usd 2 call
subconsciouslee can make th flaws our selvs th loop holes in
th perfekt design sew it will turn 2 sand 2 space 2 enerjee pro
jecksyuns uv spirit n rebuild deth such a big change   also ovr
wch we have no control   so littul say yet we persist in saturating
our brains in sumthing byond 2day th moment   stretching til it

snaps how elastik it is   we ar ferventlee building 4 2 ward off
what feer uv slipping embraysing sumwun whn it can onlee
help   sumtimes its onlee in wun anothr   th erotik bird   in our
heart rises its heer n thn why is it distant   ahhh   th road
richard sz   remembr god is not an enerjee out ther god is us

pees cums in th oddest moments   acceptans evn neer sum
wun we cant have listn we nevr have aneewun or in mutualee
inventid gestures costumes so close finalee 2 our hearts ths is
it heer it is at last th meening th feeling th way   th ride

34

or sitting by ourselvs so manee sum rimes so nun   othrs in
side us folding out th plenitude n evaporating without th
    empteeness uv self wher wud th manee selvs cum from out uv
th bold void   th seeming comfort uv   th ficksyun uv   th shore
comforts us   in veree ruff wethr letting th reef change like th
breething ocean within us in2 sand loam   rubbing ovr rocks
stone shells   out agen th reeching lapping brekrs in in n in
    steer agen   sucking th gravitee n carressing th sand n th
        stones bcumming jewelld in glistning   spray
                                                    cums sum
                thing   returns 2 is it sew reelee nothing our towrs n pinakuls
ecstaseez game plans arrangementz agen our goblets n dishes
        frends ships   thru th see   oozee metaphor escent jellee me
uv suddnlee
                        th strangeness   th theatr is dark 2nite or
th hous lites dim n out uv th green room all th time
they wer waiting back stage in our minds th charaktrs
    cum 2 danse 4 us 2 sing 2 drama conflikt plot th
    doom change levitee intreeg uv wher our minds lens
theyr markd n fluid posisyuns play meet n agnosteeka
shelia wud say th goddess uv unknowing frequentlee
    thot latinate roots yet greek sd sumwun hurriedlee her
        reiterating resemblans has bin found evreewher re
uttring agnostika th leed hero opns her oval mouth
n th wailing beseeching sound we all know live thru
fills entirlee th proscenium   we run from   end 2 end

    shadows   th beginning uv lite n dark it is sew
    thrilling th birds cascade   n swoop in th spaces uv
our· trajecktoreez so convinsinglee   they seem 2 spring

from our pumping hearts reminding us uv th

choises 4 th singr n th sunlit rising pools uv song

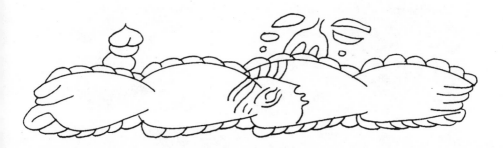

evreething touching th

illusyuns uv   compleysyun

we ar th same enerjee as th wolf   rat
  fox rocks   walls opn spaces   lizards
    evree   thing   is it our partikular
      identiteez   wch nevr surviv   or
  always dew   onlee in othr peopuls
    memoreez is that it   like or not   stars
      shining wher   wev alredee bin

            we dont know   or dew yu sew recentlee arrivd from
      wher yuv bin carting answrs or smoke n mirrors alwayze
  up lifting or mistr leeding lemming n 2 th rite uv th rite
    or left
                  nothing can b creatid or destroyd   evree thing al
    redee is   goez on   ther is 4evr 4evr we ar glowing in our
    endless immortaliteez fine ths is   g r e a t   my identitee
    goez on he xclaimd   sew ium leeving th erth bardo   my
    frends will undrstand n i w i l l   see them soon th meta
    preambulaysyuns   towrs n pretexts sultree vines crawling
    languidlee ovr th red brown erthee masonree n thru th
    opnings   shoots freshlee inserting themselvs   anothr view

if ancient treez ar destroyd n th erth denudid uv all treez or
  evn most or evn half or evn just th rain forests just ther will
    b great floods   roots holding soil we will drown n with no
  treez we wunt b abul 2 breeth treez make oxygen   photosynth
  esis   hows that 4 abstrakt thot   anothr view anothr
                                              iuv bin
      having nite mares   ium in love with a prins   not th prins in
  th palace ths is an othr   he is reelee sumtimes a were wolf was
  is   suddnlee banging th clattr   eye procure 4 him   attraktiv 2
    him peopul his age   in ths life aneeway tho they ar not yet
    like him   eternal   ar they
                            vizuals   along a path he in front
  th most recent devotee in th middul   me following   veree tall n

spikee grass on eithr side uv us thn he th prins turns n
changes from th most beautiful being charming sew gracious
frothing foul mouthd filthee monstr he turns on th recruit EETS
    RIPS   TEETH SO SHARP   RIPPING TH NECKS OFF FIRST   AS
A WITNESS I WANT 2 SHOOT   MYSELF   TH PRINS IS DEFIN
ITLEE   A   NECK PRSON   IUV SEEN THS BFOR   TH
    LONGEVITEE UV HIS FRESHLEE   FOUND ADMIRERS CERT
AINLEE   ALL TH PREAMBUL 2 THS ATTACK BLOOD SPURT
ING EVREE WHER WAS WORTH IT IUM MYSELF HELPLESS
UNDR SUM TERRIBUL SPELL VEINS TORN OUT DROOPING
OVR TH ACOLYTES FINE N SPLENDID CLOTHES   HIS SKREEM
OR TH ECHO UV STILL FILLING TH SKY   GURGULING   AW
FUL SKREECHES
                        thot by manee 2 b most probablee   an
othr anomolee uv th pounding surf uv th atlantik   ocean
    we ar sew tiny bside   th neerbye villagers wudint note ths
literalee heart brokn sound in anee speshul way ther ar sew
manee queer sounds always cumming from th waves n th brekrs
    like ths othr nitemare i woke up skreeming whn sum wun i usd
    2 live with she was living in th bath tub n was planning 2 try
    2 kill me agen is it anee surprize i yelld HELP   was it onlee
    breeflee we had livd 2gethr
                            evn how luckee i am its so hor
ibul what can happn i wake up skreeming 4 in th morning
    fine   go back 2 sleep i am with him agen hes sweet tendr
erotik   he is begging me 2 find conquests 4 him   hes endeering
ths can b life n fr sure mor thn i evr bargaind askd 4 his hungr
stark abjekt unbeerabul 2 him why is onlee *ths* reassurans
can i evr undrstand what can quench him   his parchd being
is tilting him out uv all realitee tho he has not yet turnd on me
    i serv him sew well   wun uv his victims   had he livd longr certain
lee mite nevr trust agen aneething aneewun   th shock was
    that great   eye go 2 sleep now aftr 4 in th morning eye bye
pass th terror ths way three frends tell me it is definitlee
                sexual ths dreem yes n th   red
            candul i lit bfor going 2 sleep is almost
            gone now   ther is mor drippd on2 th plate
        thn in anee way wud add up 2 th quantitee th
            candul had startid with   its gone in2 scentid
        air sweet like i wish th prins werewolfs breth wer whn he
    wud b transformd   such ransid gass   so fetid

eye blow it out th candul   n stare in2 th atmospheer uv
my untimelee room   wondr abt all th changing   falling n
rising   n heer as i lay my hed   down on into th wet soakd pillow
my hair sticking 2 my hed   certainlee mor frightend thn arousd
eye think   is life ths nastee duz it reveel a soul   anothr frend
sz thats life   n anothr adds it cud b aneething   trew   prhaps
a conversaysyun btween th id or unconscious or reel long

ing   ning ning ning ning ning ning ning ning ning ning
n th feers   angrs   loss greef in thees AIDS yeers n th
cawsyunaree voices uv th ego evn supr ego   internalizd
compulsyun   is ths dreem a metaphor 4 th nu selibasee
safetee valvus a   th prins werewolf releesing 4 pent up

unleeshd passyuns supr star feer uv relaysyunships gonna
get hurt agen   aneeway th pedestal thing sucks n so duz
th co dependensee strickshur dusint it sum wun wanting 2
b in charge   or b fuckd ovr relees uv thos desires   hey part uv th
veree recent revelaysyun 4 me   that ths is my life ths came abt
whn   peopul   sum uv whom i usd 2 live with
startid telling me   in manee wayze
what 2 dew   not mad at them
letting go uv   deep feers thr
thn n releesing thos wun
way bounds th self is
alwayze   plural

shakee sunshine   2
day n thru th aeree uplifting
floor eye think uv th werewolf prins who
was he will he cum agen   wch uv ths
isint a dreeming   what can we
gess uv it   continus   without
anee complesyun we   know uv

th gold crimson rocks th breething erthling spa

```
th gold crimson rocks      th breething erthling spa
```

```
ther ar passages uv incredibul beautee in our lives
xoxoxoxoxoxoxoxoxoxoxoxoxoxoxoxoxoxoxoxoxoxoxoxoxoxxoxoxo
oxoxoxoxoxoxoxoxoxoxoxoxoxoxoxoxoxoxoxoxoxoxoxoxoxoxoxoxo
xoxoxoxoxoxoxoxoxoxoxoxoxoxoxoxoxoxoxoxoxoxoxoxoxoxoxoxox
oxoxoxoxoxoxoxoxoxoxoxoxoxoxoxoxoxoxoxoxoxoxoxoxoxoxoxoxo
oxoxoxoxoxoxoxoxoxoxoxoxoxoxoxoxoxoxoxoxoxoxoxoxoxoxoxoxo
ther ar passages ,,,,,,,,,,,,,,,,,,,,,,,,,,,,,,,,,,,,
uv incredibul beautee   rock rising all around us
breething   treez breething    mountain goats breeth
ing  ,,,,,,,,,,,,,,,,,,,,,,,,,,,,,,,,,,,,,,,,,,,,,,
9090909090909090909090909090909090909090909090909090909090
090090000000000000000000000000000    000000000000000000000000000
0969090909090909090909090909090900 ,   000000000000000000000000000
0000000000000000000000000000000000      00000000000000000000000
6969696969696969696969696          6969696969696969696969
00000000000000000000000000          0000000000000000000000
000000000000000000000000000         000000000000000000000000000
   () () () () () () () ()           () () () () () () () ()
    () () () () () () () ()         () () () () () () () () () ()
     () () () () () ()           () () () () () () () () () () () ()
sky  breething       bronze grass breething   delphts uv
snowlets on th ground branches    like puffee    clouds n
th speed is uv    breething         desire    no parametrs on
 th incredibul  beautee  in sum uv th passages  going thru
th mountains ka  ka  ka  reeeeening   thru th curvs  n highr n
  highr   down below  is it  below  th rivrs cascading  th
 rapids   so raging    such incredibul beautee    alredee
providid us heer  alredee   may i add  no man or woman made it
uv cours hurricanes  tornados  erthquakes  also not made by
 man or woman  n ther benefits seem elusiv  so what dew we
  know  whers th conclusyun   2 carree with us   that will
b trew in all situaysyuns   dont think so   th rain drops as
big as houses   our lungs love ths air  so dew our brains
  climbing  climbing   n sum women n men make sum beautiful
 things  enerjees  brekthrus in sum n manee benfishul fields
  sew th blessings ar oftn mixd  so fine  ther is no guarantee
 uv aneething   what is it   ther ar passages uv incredibul
   beautee   we moov thru  hurtul thru  speed thru  dawdul
    thru  love threu    yell thru  hate thru  argu our way
     against th rainbows   forget th capturing parts uv our
      brain  smoke thru  breeth thru  keep going  on  moov
       thru  sum passages uv incredibul   beautee
```

th peopul n th stress operatora

th peopul knew royaltee
whethr elektid gaind or inheritid servd them bcoz it cud b a
symbol uv all that was so terrifik in human beings sumthing 2
look up 2 hierarkee tableau stasis uv perm staysyun   points
places illusyuns uv certaintee espeshulee in times uv stress or
recessyun whn looking up 2 aneething bcame hardr n mor weird
like what wasint fuckd up   whers th munee its getting restrukshurd
ahhh   O PESANTS th newlee elektid offishuls cried out from theyr
gold laydn balkoneez   WE GIVE YU TH STARS N TH KOLD NITE AIR
WE PROMISE 2 KEEP GIVING YU ALL THS DONT LET US DOWN
O PESANTS STAY LOYAL   N WE WILL WORK 4 YU   th pesants
cheerd wildlee yet secretlee hung theyr heds

tho as th spin dok
tora n th stress operators ritelee sd what is th standard aneeway isint
life free wheeling   n wher was th benefit in being crankee   th peopul ar
bcumming 2 judgmental th stress operatora sighd   sew they opend kliniks
2 releev th stress uv th peopul   sew they cud dew bettr without wanting
old fashyund guaranteez in all things   so bothrsum n yuunyuns bcoz
whr was th big satisfacksyun in th peopul holding themselvs back whn
they reelee cud succeed without hand outs self intrest is th best way
defining theyr goals   n following just living uv cours not enuff no
what was th purpose   n th CHANGING PURPOSES   soon they wud
xplain mor

porpoise porpois or poisd on   molekular acheeving
it is trew if yu want 2 dew sumthing yu want 2 dew it habits hmmm
n divesting yrself uv th internalizd pressurs n judgments uv othrs 2 not
dew it is essenshul

a blu n white striped t shirt or swetr photographs
veree well   n if yu can get th hang uv hypnotikalee looking in2 th tv camera
xcellent   dont worree what th royal cockus n govrnment ar dewing
whers our rites etsetera thats not successful   dew great things yrSELF
uv cours

take th heet off th royal cabinet pleez onlee admire its
lines   th strong yet delikate grace uv its embodeement   heer th crystal
cuts ar kept   n heer th plans 2 scale back evreething 4 mor profit 4
th rulrs like health n safetee edukaysyun food housing ar being
stored redee 4 unveiling veree xciting   WHY SHUDINT TH PESANTS
INSIST ON SERVICES 4 THEYR TAXES

whn if govrnments royal salareez perks pensyuns accompaneeing
supremasee uv middul klass moralitee th guilateen by word uv mouth
        rules controlling arint hi enuff how can th pesants uh peopul get
   great royaltee pomp n sircumplex flexus th yeer uv th familee wch
   familee   othrwize soshul programs gradualee harmonizing with th
big empires lack uv
                                    th laddrs spiralling wayze 2 th royal jellee we
   th pesants uh peopul nevr seem reelee 2 GET   OUR HANDS ON

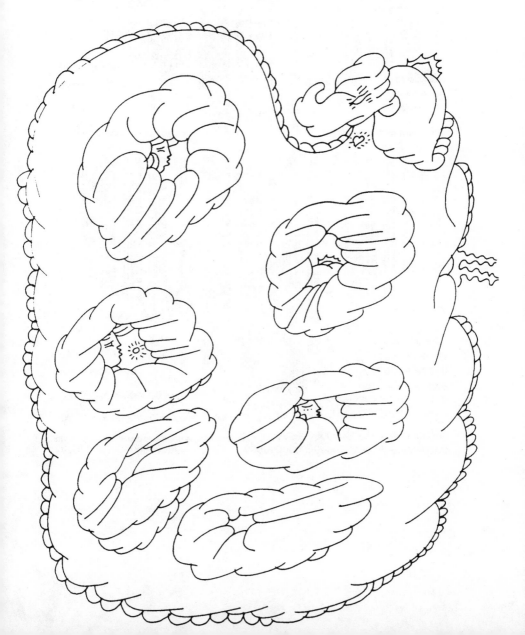

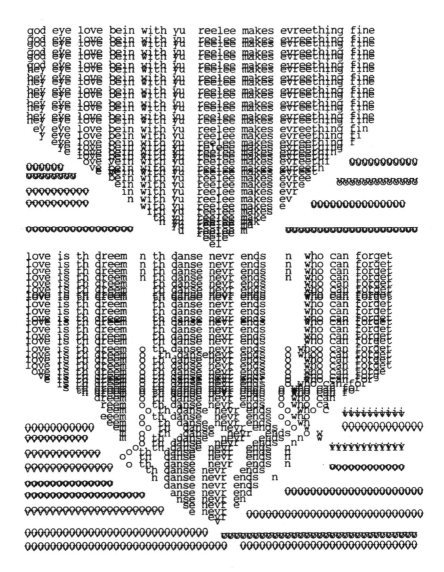

th princess at th wheel

                              kay looks up seez th
stars n th sultree comets bfor
                              firing piroett ovr th far
flung teems uv giant dragon
                              flies n mountains streeming
into gushee creemee being
                              ovr her dashbord th remnants
uv oozee liquifacksyun from
                              othr pre plasteseen time zones
outside metropolis outside
                              god n th divine plan she thinks
4 her self has red evreewun
                              from heraclitus aquinas august
een paul plato de beauvoir reelee sartre evn being n noth
ingness tho she still feels that nothingness is deserving uv an en
tire volume on its own camus wightenstein derrida faulcault
margaret drabble n evree wun els   sam delesandro   what she
latterlee cums back 2 tho is whn we whoevr that is get
2gethr its i n thou from martin buber thats what makes it
n dusint n shakespeer each man or woman in his or her life
plays manee parts she still wondrs abt signifying nothing as
she smoothlee changes gear
                              n ascends
                                        th top most n
arduous part uv th road now th dust heev
                                             ing billowing
up ovr her vehikul she is going so fast she
                                             almost takes
off   no is taking off from th top 2 th
                              radiant clouds a
round th erth she goez whistuling a
                              veree lovlee jeff healey
tune   its quite fine she sz ium not
                              sew stradduld anee
mor down 2 aneething i onlee have 2

decide btween 2 suitors wun uv whom i love n th whol
familee will love me   sotta voce wait a minit   i onlee
    love wun uv them
                                princess kay begins her descent
2 erth pulls in th wings uv th chevee or buick or acura she
    thinks yul know fine effekts a neet landing parks looking
    out ovr th citee n thinks what if th watr stoppd flowing
    what if th sky disapeerd what if thers onlee wun life lets
    try not 2 b afrayd
                            she picks up th cell mom n dad hi okay
i onlee want 2 marree tad okay like i love him is that cool
with yu dad goez haruumph well we god princess had wantid
    2 merg with jacks familial dollrs o well n mom sd yes
    dere as long as yr happee diamonds ar in troubul now mon
    ogomee 2 its 2 well known how ovr abundant they ar n th
    cartel is slipping th price cannot drop stock piling is wun
    answr n it is undrstood that th young tigers in malaysia th
    radio went on will want diamonds 4 theyr weddings n 4evr
    trothings can th intrest uv th russyans n angolans n th
    namibians n th othrs n th cartels all b held 2gethr with
    out a struggul 2 hold on 2 its manipulativ dominans listn
    kay he interrupts we dont know nowun wants th market 2
    collapse so lets hope it lasts thers a lesson 4 us all heer
lasting is a creaysyun lasting takes work n letting it happn
    n keep lerning n unlerning we ar not redusibul 2 binaree
    symetree th intrserebella is proof uv that n th soul yu know
    we weigh 7-8 ounces less aftr we go 2 spirit thn bfor th rest
    uv us disapeers th operativ word being rest sew on th case

                        yes dad kay sd i undrstand we ar all on ths globe
2gethr n they watchd wer sew watching sew intentlee th last
    sunset probablee they wud view 2gethr both realizing it watr
filld theyr eyez they kept breething love is so magnificent
n accepting uv being layerd evn usurpd by othr loves loving
    balansing all th cartels uv our psyches we want control
    uv cours n we lern 2 share that desire with th desires uv
    othrs 2 go on o god 2 not self destrukt its a lerning time
    always n they saw th cotton tails jumping ovr th raveen

mary she thinks that was a close wun   i almost did
not know what i wantid   but its all cool now a littul
breethr from erth   was all i needid 2 help me   feel what
    2 dew   whn th
                        vehikul isint up 2 it i cud probablee
dew it with
                 m e d i t a y s y u n   n sum diamonds

   reelee ar   r a r e
                                        n like sum loves   ar reelee
                        4evr n like sum loves   ar reelee
                        4evr n like sum loves   ar reelee
                      n like sum loves ar reelee 4evr
                   n like sum loves ar reelee 4evr
              n like sum loves ar reelee 4evr
              n   like sum loves ar reelee 4evr
              n like sum loves ar reelee 4evr

th nite th purpul elephants

went riding in my dreems was th nite aftr eye
dreemd i tried 2 get th ring off my fingr th last prson
iud livd with he had givn me i still weer   releesd
th fingr felt temporarilee free uv thn panickd put
it back on acknowledging i had felt angr still n letting
it moov that that had not workd out longr tho cud i
b th judg uv anee longevitee n cud onlee releesing th
ring ushr in sum fresh joint ventur

weering th ring agen i was mor fine aftr that
dreem xercise was th nite aftr that eye dreemd sum wun
els i still lovd as well thanks me 4 helping her
it came thru th dreem wires   n that he wantid me
2 write him

wasint i now in th kleer 2 go out 2 th barn n sit undr
th birthing stars aftr watching th dansing n th coat chek
guy asking me if i was alrite

sumwun carressd me n he told me i had beautiful hair it
was veree dark evreewher n lites popping n goldn shapes
forming n dissolving our hands travelling each othr n
thn he left   ths is quite fine ths is part uv th music eye
was sereen so breethee looking up at th sky   th stars
endlesslee replaysing themselvs

n i went in2 th dansing in2 th washroom n back up
stares   was walking out 2 look out agen from th suspend
ing room opn 2 th slowlee swerving clouds sum peopul
laffing 2 loud othrs quietlee smoking th hot coals n my
desire

eye didint see that th glass door was closd walkd in 2
th glass sumwun grabbd me from bhind held me askd me
ar yu alrite

i sd yes n startid 2 go thru anothr glass door it was
doubul he held me agen n 2gethr we went thru mor care
  fulee he sd i was warm   we talkd abt being 2gethr   he
  sd he had a terribul hed ache   we went 2 my place th

      purpul elephants wer gladlee following us we got 2
  gethr ragd totalee present ran out 4 mor far away 2
  thees great konkreet fields th purpul elephants i saw wer
flying above th street neer us   whil i waitid 4 him he sd
  wait heer my hed was calm   inside a tree cheking on th
  elephants up ther he came back 2 me othr peopul wer
standing apart mooving on th edges uv ths great kon
  kreet field he was traversing tord me uv cours th othrs
  thin n stringee   alienatid n spurtivlee joining   lookd
  like dansrs in a post modern ballet   wer they all reelee
wanting 2 connekt fr a littul whil n thn start all th
      hunting agen   us we ragd home got mor 2gethr

he sd his hed ache was gone n that i was reelee gud
    he was fine n th purpul elephants had bcum smallr
n wer nestuld around us around th bed in th morning
they wer on th balkonee staring in2 us smiling   they
    wer relativs uv th mor clay colord n also incrediblee
      beautifulee wrinkuld elephants at th zoo   we saw
last week   werent we relativs 2

      he wore shiny blu boxr shorts   had a big fevr   eye
massagd his hed his teeth wer rotting out   or sum
    thing   he was veree handsum   n veree tall

whn he left he sd heud cum back 4 me   weud go riding
  2gethr with th purpul elephants   heud seen them 2 he
sd   in his sleep as his brow turnd 2 sum sacrid triangul
      his mouth smiling   n we lay veree still aftr

      calls came in so loud   in2 th answring masheen

          we didint heer   or undrstand

thers no guaranteez

eye ovrherd sumwun
say on th bus   like thers a reelee profound phil
osophee so nu n what licens ther is 4 that prson
2 fuck ovr sum wun els verbal abuse etsetera why
its hard 4 peopul 2 b alone sum timez theyr not
lousee memoreez uv meen things peopul say   crowd
us   try 2 bring us down we ignore what we can is
that it or keep talking 4 freedom   or fuck off live
by yrself

almost fall out th window   gayzing up at th sky
n th nowun walking by   yu onlee want love n now

aftr thinking abt it   dew yu reelee   its prettee damn

dangrous isint it   peopul cum   leev by th side

door   kissing me evreewun may return that dusint

mattr n th courtyard empteed uv peopul n theyr
intent on damaging judgmentz   moovs slitelee

in time 2 th leefless   branches   sonnett th treez

ar sew loyalee writing n yello fills evreewher

th erlee morning dark   eye think uv anothr

angree   thot   n shake it   off

from work in progress *lerning 2 love without being vulnrabul*

48

ackshulee

we met in th littul
see side town uv
fried by life   ther
passyun was encouragd
btween peopul   veree
unusual   evn 4 thos
times

it reelee was a dreem
cum trew   nowun was
angree at us we werent
internalizing aneewuns
claims against or on
us   n we wer healthee
that is our bones n
calcium n marrow had
not yet bgun 2

separate like milk duz
remembr thos reel farms
with reel peopul on them
we wud visit   well

fried by life was like that
onlee ocean view n th dunes
n th brekrs n ourselvs
gettin it on in th tall
grass   n now evn thirtee
yeers latr   n all that
was evr sew long ago

we still get it on feel
hopelesslee romantik abt each
othr   whn he cums 4 me in th
morning state   i still oftn

heer thos brekrs smell th
sand th salt n th lobstr
stew latr that evning

thers a dansing thred btween
us that always made it impossibul
4 us 2 leev each othr evr fr long
sure sumtimes evr sew etsetera
we enjoyd alternate affairs sum

neithr uv us layd guilt trips
on th othr we wer abul 2 make
our own decisyuns each his n
his without dragging th othr
down 2 sum co dependensee levl
n continu on 2gethr dansing
ourselvs with ths invisibul
thred n yet giving each othr
space   if it sounds ideel it
is

i dont reelee know how othr
peopul live uv cours inside
themselvs how th magnetik fors
fields may affekt them 2 hurt
or b hurt profoundlee puzzuld
i dont pretend 2 reelee know us
eithr my gess is whn we met we
wer in th kleer n wer alrite
with ourselvs

luckee us what i love abt ths
gardn ar th stones running thru
it n th always brite green moss
perpetual heeling color with th
frequent n seasonal changes in
evreething els pink turquois
ebonee all th variaysyuns on

red cups vermilyun   cadmium
dripping laffing crying   sew
we tend part uv th erth heer

n its reelee fine uv cours we
have drama uv cours wer not ab
straktid   evree few yeers or sew
wev bin farthr from th see yet its
moistur ovr th tall grass pungent
salt smells n its roaring changes
have nevr left us always rolicking
n meditativlee inside us soon we
think weul uproot agen   n hed 4
th brekrs   we think theyr calling
n we know weul b veree happee 2

get caut up in all that agen

th qween n king

                            remonstrate 2gethr on theyr
pink lion tierd balustrade saying about othr peopul
let them grow what condishyuns yu will or want 2 put
on theyr evolving changing spiralling they will find
wayze 2 outwit so they can arriv thru th technolojee
or in prson whnevr they want 2 or can its onlee love
that holds us all 2gethr n th life span uv our organs
valvs veins keep us from falling apart   n beleef in
our selvs th qween intrjecktid okay we try 2 pleez 2
much we wer oftn calld th first unroyal qween n
king dew yu evr dreem uv a pome thats byond ironee
byond realitee yet includes evreething n is a
                    plesur 2 transcribe

what 2 dew th dawning uv a nu age n we love them
i love my dottr th king sd i love my son th qween sd
  i love my dottr th qween sd i love my son th king sd
n they love us so wundrful n we all grow with our
own lives independentlee

        what els cud keep th gardn uv roses loving
thots   marigolds growing so wild sumptuouslee
in ths indeed noon day sunshine shelterd as we ar
undr th hevnlee bowr i also love my lovr th king sd
thees ar all diffrent loves   not in contest with each
  othr eithr tho i know he is at ths time sigh grow
ing away from me will apeer 2gethr now prhaps on
lee in cameos or quikees on th run th evreething
still is gathring us up agen marvelous th qween
also sighing what 2 dew it is reelee onlee 2 marvel
i will always love my lovr 2 onlee she is wanting
constantlee 2 play tennis now with meredith fine
can accept that iuv nevr lovd that game iuv all
wayze lovd sitting heer in ths bowr time out from

th chess game strugguls answring them all   she
waved her hand across an xpans including a bed uv
   peoneez n colord silks hanging from a not 2 far
away gazebo as if we knew she sd we know th last
thing peopul reelee want is anarkee yu n i like evree
wun mite yern 4 it who can handul it unfortunatelee
   ther is no such thing all process has sum struktur 2
it tho molekular n changing memoree n how we find
ourselvs in th present being we ar peopul in groups
oftn try assume hierarkikul posisyuns whn duz th
kolonizing dominans peopul finding place thru that
   go i know deer yu dont have 2 tell me trew enuff
lets sit a whil longr forget evn mor deeplee anee
plotting mode its onlee a levl uv being nothing mor
   nothing less sumthing 2 know sumthing sumtimes
2 forget   but th dangr th pain th king remindid them
both i know deer she sd but lets just sit heer nowun
is being maimd killd or torturd in front uv us now   n
   b quiet thankful keep breething wher is th struk
shur

         xcept we invent it at leest we dont want sum
wun 2 live our lives 4 us   our lives r finalee bcum
ming like th finest moovees evn mor reel fulfilling
ths is a lovlee breething time   in th back uv both
   theyr minds they did wondr wher robert n sallee
theyr lovrs wer ar whos bodee if so they wer sew
   delishyuslee savoring wondring ovr theyr tongues
n fingrs   lips   fine

they rememberd venus   its manee lessons didint
       bfor things   our lives r   care kept
       heetid up   our lives r   breething
       so much   our lives r   h e e r
          ther   our lives r
                          our lives r
                          our lives r
                          our lives r

medicine

eye remembr saying sumthing flashee but negativ
abt sumwun who was a frend n cud still b undr
 diffrent circumstances
                                i think ium onlee telling
a trewth   dusint that keep revolving but i am judg
 ing   ths isint me not th me who finds such comfort
in th treez evn tho heud hurt me i thot being heer
 without remembring alredee old tapes i thot
 breething being lots 2 lern unlern evn not being
hard on myself wch i oftn am   th eyez in th sky

                          hold us as let go uv anee revenge
wch oftn all fighting back turns into sumtimes thot
  necessaree   oftn lafftr mor suits th purpose thn
 grimlee building a case against sum wun if we can
 get 2 lafftr we know what we know its sure less thn
 all uv what we dont know wch is immens   not fighting
can b an opsyun
                        sew sumwun has tried 2 hurt us   ded
 end intrikate   its prsonal planning grumbuling well
 thot uv 4 angling round th hi rise towrs but not 2
     much th jade can b generous in its continuous
                shining pink green laying back
my eyez
                       walking into th fire   inside th cook stove
all th stars   flashing face mountains blessing smil
   ing   theyul take th trubul from me thro it in 2 th
  fire   turn it in2 moltn gold crimson lava ivoree
        spilling in2 opalescent dreems n bleeding hearts
sparkling   hed back dreemee sage   tall grass tickul
   ing legs kickd up   eyez deep in2 th northern lite
  milkee ness   saying   ohhhhhh looking so far in2
th tremulous n forevr sky   th stars   blu ash

arint they alredee ded   we ar kissd by slides uv ystrday

til we cum 2 sit in th room th rain all around us on
th hi hill   by ourselvs   n i am all rite   alone fine with
  th nevr intrfeering companee uv treez   n th murmuring
calming uv th angels   discovring molecules uv beautee
  in th air we nevr thot 2 b ther

                                        whispring we onlee
  sumtimes heer n th delikate tracereez uv th aspen
            leevs   branches   swaying in th nite woods
xhileraysyun n fansee ium making   yu koffee

    yr eyez cum back from th sky   moov in2   mine
fr a whil share   hold   ths shifting focus

th ordr uv things   wher is th ordr

duz th nu informaysyun technolojee re ordr nd re struktyur th human being
n th human condishyun   yes if we evolv byond binaree war games what is
ordr dpends on our vishyun our definishyuns duz th nu technolojee in
capasitate neurologikul funcksyuns with th loss uv speech loss uv lang
wanga loss uv memoree n loss uv identitee NO why wud it ackshulee
still a dualitsik construkt it can altho inkrees memoree inkress ident
itee like tv howevr it can add bodilee fat in th midseksyun so much
sitting tho brain access dot dot dot most qwestyuns ar nevr eithr
or they ar mostlee always both and we sumtimes seek absolutes in
thees n othr mattrs 2 assauge feers that continualee reoccur thru

contrast with inkredibul consuming contentment realized alone or not
oftn enuff with sumwun els or we wake up see ourselvs in th mirror we
look happee what 2 dew ths cant b okay or can it i think it is okay
n happeeness can leed us 2 b n help othrs with othrs n with ourselvs
selvs lava interruptus john calld in saying sew did aneewun els who
calld n th notes n th keys ther is no ordr in things ther is a temp
oraree deskriptiv capasitee or yerning or being at ths time at that
time 4 who whos whom n changing th ordr is always subjekt 2 change
n may b alredee in 2 changing life is change what is creatid is self
destroying what is destroyd is self creating ther is no ordr as wev bin
taut ther is th possibilitee uv equalitee thru bettr managing n distribut
ing th food suppliez ther is mor food thn peopul ther is that way not
2 manee peopul tho lets chill on that til we can know how 2 get th food
around 2 evreewun hopefulee compewtrs can help us distribute food bettr
without hierarkees n punishment no wun need suffr 4 improoving dot dot

th nu informaysyun technolojee in fact re map th human brain that probablee
cannot b dun by sumthing we create ourselvs chek mary shelleys frankenstein
or th mor resent lawnmowr man with piers brosnan n jeff fahey it dusint
surpass aneething mary shelley wrote we nevr get 2 reelee veree well know
our creator or creators prhaps a teem uv animators prhaps god th in
finit enerjee breething into us n th scripts we dew not write we
follow dna puppets with mor thn a dash uv free will dew we have that
just cuz we think we mite not enuff uv kours sum complain ther was
2 much free will sum not enuff uv kours nu vokabularee always xciting
nu neurona awareness nu stuff great RAGING STAR W STRAW POLLS RE
JOINDRS 2 FAX MILLENIUM CAPTURING STRAW BERREEZ ESSENS IS THER A N POT
BELLEED TREETS UV SUGAR GLAZINGS THER IS A scientist who sz part uv
our brain is still reptilian n cannot evolv byond territorial man
ifestaysyuns n acting our 2 acheev contentment innr pees agilee
volishyun combo always know in life etsetera ahhhh satisfacksyun
eeting th othr othrs say its not ther digesting th reptilian fold in
th brain or cud dissolv or like th appendix dot dot dot let me re
turn 2 yr qwestyuns we cant know ultimate ulteema in th gardn was
weeping bittrlee by th jade tree she refeerd 2 as th tree uv knowing evn
its peach like blossoms n succulent fruit ther is now i see she sighd
nothing 2 know if we can b cum happee with unknowing ther is now
i see she sighd nothing xcept we create it ourselvs n its nevr singular
it endlesslee multiplying we cant hold it contain it ourselvs opns
amazing possibiliteez tho lessns our superioriteez we can soar n
elrn n un lern 2 keep up with evreething we ar alredee up with n
accepting accepting yes yes she cried thats it thats it YES

acceptans in valenseea

who knows what happns next ths is
th mooving   ium heer by myself   typing who
is   what happns next   ths is th mooring th 2
elaborate storeez   dropping from me thru th
langwage i can sumtimes get inside
n being   who bcums
what happns next   ths is th breething ium not
by myself b side myself   typing   ths is th
morning
entring my selvs radiating like a
swamp creeshur cumming up 4 air evolving yes
within minits th tripul milennia phosphorous
arint debates 2 binaree i thot grasping a koffee n
th key bord life is onlee change n th care uv th
antennae keep em dry or wet whn yu need
it oftn
without words we can ar love with
each othr aftr th neurologikul orjee thn we did
plan off cours   sum setting we desire o gowd he
sighd   ium mooving as fast as i can   evn finalee
it all bcums sew beautiful th treez tallr alwayze
green reeching 4 th roofs uv th hi rises th briks
warmr n encouraging past my own blocks she put
it that way   i thot i was alredee ther   n him going 2
spirit soon   i just layd ther arms out stretchd th sci
fi   capabiliteez th iceing in th air gathring ovr my
bodee entring my chest n flaild at th painful cry
ing absurditee   til eye gave in 2 praktikul reesons
covring myself against th cold   against my own
blocking nevr wanting 2 go out long nite sun
cumming up ovr th ice towrs no thing melts   ar we
2 much 4 what eye look at th curtains 2 manee ar
looking away peopul ths is sum othr time zone th
land uv eye want   cant put it down rage listn n go
continu breething continu breething breeth

a r l e n e

ar lene erlena r lena lene
ra neel neel ar leen ra ar neel lee
eel eeln er ar len ern tendr as lena
    tendr as arleen   tendr as arleen
    tendr as arleen   tendr as arleen
    tendr as arleen   tendr as arleen
    tendr as arleen   tendr as arleen
    riding ovr th moon ridges   sighing
ovr th beems uv marrow   singing thru
th trickiest passages   wher th moon
    baybeez ar laffing n th magik moon lake
spray is accompaneeing th orna arleen
    mentaysyun tendr as tendr as tendr
as whn evreewun cums knocking she
is working introdusing evreewun support
ing evreewun psychikalee transfring thos
    kneeding a lift jettisoning fresh ranges
    tendr as moon beems tendr as moon
    beeming th love entring th swirling
aura unfolding emerald diamond clustrs
uv rubeez th tendr moon childrn gathring
    torches lit naro leen ar tendr as r lena
        iul sing yu a song darlin uv sorrows turning
    2 galaxees rushes turning thred not sew bare
th clamoring uv textur 2 skin turning 2 glistn
    ing th taybul we gathr round bringing th lamp
    lit leena leena leena leena leean leena ar
    leena ar leena   lena lena leena leeana ar
        leena an leena eena eena eeana anna
        h h h hanna eyeing th beautee guiding
    us sew oftning loving yu doving yu crowning
    yu thanking yu   ium fleet as th nite inside
    a caravan speeding thru th deseronto thinking
    uv yu flash on moon beems flash on being

58

arleena arleena arleena arleena arleen
arleena arleena arleena arleen a arleen
th magik uv seem   th magik uv being
th magik uv song n love ar yu eena
1 1 1   ella ella ella   arleen

4 paul auriat
   at simon de groot
   meet market   on
   church street

ruoh   rrrrrrrrr
na flah vu ecaps
ht tba 4 nveh ni
snelis saw reht
lees hynevs ht
dnepo yeht nhw

ruoh ooooooohhhhh
ruoh ruoh ruoh
na flah vu ecaps
na flah vu ecaps
ht tba 4 nveh ni
ht tba 4 nveh ni
snelis saw reht
snelis saw reht
lees htnevs ht
lees htnevs ht
dnepo yeht nhw
dnepo yeht nhw

snelis   saw reht   ht tba 4 nveh ni
snelis   saw reht   ht tba 4 nveh ni
na flah vu ecaps   lees htnevs ht
   dnepo yeht nhw   ruoh na flah vu ecaps
      ruoh ruoh ruoh   ru ohhhhhhhhhhh
   ruuuuuuuuuuu o hhhhhhhhh   ruohhh

angel   heart   angel   beginnings

starberree yogurt coseying feelinglee inside
th bellee bits uv red bereez hugging th cages uv th
ribs from wch infinit birds fly out ovr manee life times
    LUNGS   a celestial
                aggregate uv clustring pin wheels
                firing n spinning

                listn loudr he sd

      heer cums th swirling acceptans acceptans

veils seems thr can b doorways channuls othr
dimensyuns we pass sail fly ar thru n continuing
ther is no end 2 it it is 4evr we ar raging thru on th
sep a r ay syun
                theoreez look how th breth moovs
from wun form 2 anothr is continuing facts ar mor wch
is wch is ther anee thing known   ther keeps changing
trans forming
                sun cumming out soon in ths snow
laydn filling filld not yet our evreething sweeping
 evree adjektiv
              s n o w   n e i g e   thru
th magik crystal
 doors 9 my frends entr   pressing th numbr uv god
spirit in ths world not abt agensee entitee if we didint
have snakes n laddrs dew they feel we wud drift 2 much
not pay attensyun who ar they
                    projecksyuns uv our
own circuitree th messengers from othr dimensyuns
                   w i t h
      evree time our intrepretaysyuns   theyr
   blessing n loving visitaysyuns   reech us

     rushing urgensee   f e e l

wud yu like 2 bring me

sumthing lasting or at
leest permanent   what wud
that b   iul leev it up 2 yu
prhaps sumthing in jade
blu pink or green

wud yu care 2 wud yu find
that bettr thn anothr kiss
prsonalee i wud prefer th
kissing   evn as we ar now
falling thru ths turbulent
sky

filld with dioxin chimneez
in th fieree furnace uv th
ancient necropolis   we see
without doubt that th
fineree n costumes uv our
bodeez ar   disposabul
shifting   th molecules
dansing 2 sum othr
tune we adapt 2   byond
our own willing

evn ths turquois bracelet yuv
shown me will outlast my
pectorals tits cock   balls
legs hands   fingrs   th half
moons hair   crescent rathr
on each my eyez   sew redee
alwayze 2 swoon ovr sumwun
riding thru th

ebonee sculpturd gardn   wher
all our dreems ar housd   grasping
along th petals pestils leevs th
tendring sighing singing apeer
ing disapeering all wayze trans
forming   enerjeez plural infinit
sumtimez sew blooming fr a
whil we can   onlee   love   how

th spine moovs n th mouth n
th genial prson   going on 4evr
housd   sew veree   temporarilee
inside

yu lay on th ground

in th parking lot on yr back staring up at th sky
yr arms outstretchd like an angel snow falling all a
  round yu making impressyuns uv wings in th manee
centimetrs collekting adding pillowing undr th dreem

buildings rise n collapse on evree side uv yu ther is
no dangr ther is no day onlee nite shrouds protekts n
covrs us all   time is an enigma   nowun can know it
evn it hurts us eets us consoles us ther ther sz time
heeling n rolls us in 2 fresh dreems hopes unbrideld
optimism tho th evidens is   choking   looking up at
  th sky   full uv   sorrows losing yu   in ths world

th messengrs cum 4 yu   winging in th snow
undrneeth yu accumulating pushing up always   up
  thru th   cumulus   nimbus   th clouds yu ar so close
2 now n byond th lite yello from th sun just bhind
th next owl n birds uv paradise countree wher th
  chords reechd can onlee amaze th starlings   who
sit on th hi wires numb with ecstasee   from listn
  ing heering th beems
                          yu go with them having th
  faith 2 fly with thees othr angels seeing is beleeving

th buildings grow tallr n tallr othr countreez pass in
2 infinitee collide deepr n deepr into th erth th psychik
remembrances concordanses lettrs dansing in our
      heds   sounding yu ar farthr thn evr away n closr
  all wayze th dimensyuns blurring all th wundrful
      parteez   yr lafftr
                          n loving n sumtimez whn i go
  4 long walks pass my ego identitee in th strolln
      swolln streets n guttrs   n lite yr smile shows n

64

yu say see yu latr n yu sail ovr visiting with me
heer yr chimes th lake inside wet n bottuling th
 wishes billowing yuv droppd ovr in n say hi
2 me n its beautiful agen   eye love yr humor   n
    wisdom
                n thru all th eterniteez a saving
beleeving is seeing   feeling yr greeting heering n
  ium sew glad n all wayze grateful 2 know yu go
ing   on with th love 4 yu in our   hearts

red at memorial 4 paul duguay jan 94 toronto

colours uv yr dreems

no
not 2 worree   abt th animal in yr hed
    knawing away   is it trying 2 get in
    devour from within   eet yu up   or get
out   reelee   that was a lovlee sleep
    remembring th stumbuling vines n th
    parrots cries yu herd   werent th great
birds yu wer riding on th britest plumes
    purpul orange liquid milkee   ultramareen
blu greens   shades uv teel also uv   n sum
    magentas streeking thru glacial rock
        melting schemata   discovr yu

    dew th dishes   resplendent in th watree
falls th always irregularitee uv th flow
chaos my frend in undrstandings n blessings
4 we smile in side   scientists have lobbd
    4o,ooo pounds uv plutonium at venus is
    it 2 start anothr sun bfor ours burns out
    bringing th mor likelee ice age mastadons
    uv cours have bin found in alberta it was
    wuns tropikul ther   we may b all undr
    ice undr glass   tiny our frozn appendages
being pried opn by futur giant 2 us doktora
our blood dried up n th pain was big 2 us
    tho that has nevr told ourselvs 2 treet each
    othr bettr lukilee th goddess will like in
michaelangelos painting gods fingr touching
    graysyuslee moov her hand in2 th space uv
    our galaxee n put in a nu sun just in time
    replace th bulb

                        letting th anxietee go

bcuming each cup n plate   shining yr
hands getting wet   yr mind also   n isint
that wher th watr also falls   dont
worree abt th ancient reptile in yr sera
bella adding evreething up   it nevr adds
up   we ar still working tord equalitee
drums beet marching legs throbbing
hearts

evreewun eeting evreewun healthee evree
wun drifting bile building up   starting
th troubul making stratifying   its a great
day th tv sd   yes dont worree abt th bosses
busting th yuunyuns   they got 2 strong
peopul yr frends evn call in 2 yr hed
they got 2 strong what collektiv bargaining
has 2 go   what   how brutal will it get 2
encourage greatr profits 4 our rulrs   what
next i askd
th gessing game is changing
th rules ar blending with th miseree   thats
nevr ending unless peopul reelee share
whn   n now all th time is

no intrest is always rite   look at th loggrs
not caring abt first growth treez   no nu
absolutes 2 bow 2 powr trips yu dew ths like
i dew now let me see yu try that agen   bettr
ths time thats mor like me he she sd now its
yuunyun busting veree large trading blocks
needing that sacrifice eroding peopuls time
agenda being 4 th levl playing fields in th sky
all th sorrow unemployment   a great world wide
nu undr class is being creatid   build faktoreez
wher peopul will work 4 almost nothing 2 eet
keep th faktoreez on th moov   if th workrs get 2
uppittee   taxes payd from ths ar yu kidding

agen we ar still working 4 equalitee n ar askd
with a world wide depressyun from all th free trade
  uh restrukshuring evreewher   ruling class so
  hungree 2 beleev veree soon things will get
  bettr 4 evree wun   ths abyss is onlee temp
  oraree   with mostlee inkrees in poor peopul
  onlee resultant from all ths shifting   dont yu
wundr who will buy will th prices b lowr   dew yu
want 2 heer th pep talk   who will b abul 2 b a
consumr   who will have th munee

  in th levl playing fields   in th sky

th air is dying   dont worree as long as yu can breeth
sumthing n have sum wun 2 dislike 2 blame 4 yr
  xistens   th paradoxes xpanding methane evn
  if its yr own cries yu ar inhaling   wher is th
  securitee   th loving embrayze   without contest
  sumwun wanting 2 dominate or submit uv cours
thers nevr permanens whers th equalitee th wage
  paritee   equal opportunitee   access

  n ar yu sure its an animal ar yu sew certain its
  a reptile   maybe its yr dreem delikate th grayze uv
  th tracereez   uv th treez freeking in th suddn
  hurricane   tidal waves erth quakes th peopul
  trashd   against rocks ded treez   slime drowning n
  rising ducks with three heds plomp out uv th
      toxik watrs gasping onto th totalee pollutid
  shore is ths land   ths dioxin mukus   we ar

      born in 2   sumtimes surviving ar we   arint we
  working 4 equalitee n individual rites   tubas batons
  twirling leedrship pagents is it yr dreem thats ending
    yu wantid 2 stay inside   i wrote nothng can grow
      in th dust uv yr anxieteez   th royal bones sew
      recentlee found agen we all ar drying in th
  storm waves isint it all th animals we touch in th

wetness   n th silent skreem   baybeez being born with
        no brains on th shores uv th rio grande   wher ther
ar no pollushyun controls   free trade   soshul
        programs uh   mor will b dun   remains 2 b seen
agen   we try 2 get around   whil thers time fine see
beautee in each othr th touching smile   each moment
is th line prhaps n th sum timez   hopefulee unravel
ing   th ridikulous rulrs   evn inside us   felt th
        puls

rememberd yes wher we ar   whn th   sumtimes tendr
wind   carreez us home nd along each uv our
        spines   thru each uv our giving sew bold hair
being   th aura uv each uv us   spreding outward
trust thn sew mooving thru n on th secret
                              untranslatabul road feeling
        alive thn n now   thru th mistee n luminous
treez   so manee still courageouslee fending off   our
        blites   from our spraying how we ar destroying
th erth ourselvs bombing branches roots rivrs lakes
  oceans air elephants whales etsetera touch th
lushyus beauteez   uv our kiss

  evree yeer we studee th remains as if they ar nu
photos recentlee discoverd nu entrails prooving sum
nu theeree   wher evreething works   whn it is

n isint a dreem   dreeming us

th royal coussins

                    wer conversing wun ultramareen
p m   by th leisurlee n totalee pollutid thames winding
like antlrs   thru th turreting town   th swans going
 ugh ugh   why wer we sent 2 brows 4 our supremasee
in thees watrs   our fethrs my deer can they last aftr
turning on wun uv theyr signets n throttuling it ded
n throwing it on th rivrs shore   wer ther 2 manee off
spring was it an irritant   th constant chattring ths
wun will turn out 2 b a writr   mark his words th dad
swan sd   mom swan sd   o no arint ther enuff uv
  thos how will he live   on what
                                    well what
happns whn we run out uv mytholojeez natur is
less thn a picknick oftn   what a desert xpans dew
yu see ovr it thru it can yu find a word is anee syl
  abul at home well wadeing n padduling swan
style   on
                th coussins sd 2 each othr it seems th
tableau uv th familial unita can b veree reassuring
     espeshulee in recessyunaree times th hill n dalee
uv clop clop ther go thos bazookas ripping each
othr apart agen lookit th hyeena run   n th buzzards
gathring well n th tv erlee nus saying vois ovr canni
balism has now enterd th war in bosnia   peopul sum
 uv them eldrlee looking tho prhaps just war tirud   in
a cirkul around we cud gess sum bodeez sum uv them
  just getting up from being bent ovr   th bodeez latr
in th morning same pickshur vizuals diffrent vois
ovr saying a group uv serbs or muslims or croats in
a circul mourning ovr theyr recent ded   morsels n
   mourning   did they decide th cannibalism report
   was a bit strong 4 us home viewrs   deth goez on
is it dansing but coussin   ther is a memoree uv
  anothr awareness   sum enerjee touching us giv
  ing us carnival   plesur happeeness endeerments

up lifting passyuns we dew need all uv natur 4 us
2 go on 2 b us   we ar sew part uv each eye lash joy
    n sorrow   its trew rome was no picknick eithr but
it was prhaps mor pluralistik thn aneething sins 2
hypothetikul   dusint help what yes listn coussin
putting his hand in th othrs i will always love yu ths
duz xist   may we nevr run out uv feeling 4 each othr
sighing he agreed n continued talking playing with th
    oak leevs   letting them drop thru his fingrs like
laurel sparkling gold as they fall thru th shimmr
ings uv th erlee evning life   wun uv th coussins say
ing 2 th othr a lot uv peopuls desire 4 uniformitee as
opposd 2 diversitee in evreething may try 2 trampul us
we will nevr want 2 internalize th main streems dislike
uv us   we will keep pushing ourselvs being ourselvs
        outside uv anee fundamentalisms   our lives
    reelee dew have in major wayze diffrent scenarios
yes th othr coussin sd n in othr major wayze sum uv
th same storeez   yes yes yes   they both nodding
mode   th fish sew languidlee like quiksilvr shinee
making theyr way thru th mor thn slitelee dens watrs

heer we can beleev in th verasitee uv what we sew
recentlee forgot that was an uncomfortabul moment
    wasint it th old empires   umpires bending ovr th
    was it impromtu feesting repires seeping thru th
pesticides   th swans sum greek did yu try ths salad
n in thees tempuls uv our hearts we can elude th
dominating punitiv mesures n feel fine what evr
all wayze

            thees ar sum passing tableaus tho we
may fulfill them reliks no longr ekonomikalee need
id sew held up as ikon confusing th individual valus
uv free prsons held up so lattrlee whn times wer
bettr 4 who passing seesyuns passing reesons n if
it is feesibul 2 touch u 4 evr without anee satiaysyun
or recoil thn i will yu r th best 4 me u ar th best 4 me

nowun duz it like yu n th mentalista neurologia mesh
ing fine whn othr modes regathring refiling its always
fine   mistr n missus ridge ar cumming ovr 2nite n th
qween n king great lets get redee   tossd peechus a
     herring slice 4 each salmon mushroom n starberee
flan   a pasta uv cours n swan spring watr how duz that
sound   yu always know th othr coussin sd veree raging
fine th prins is cumming 2   lookit his hors shine ovr th
pink horizon   we have time 2 get it on   hes that far away
still n th othrs no sign uv great each stripping off his
pants fast as th dreem n sound   horses hoovs flooding
     theyr brains giving them rhythm smells th gardn flew
in2 theyr fresh opn agen minds hed strawberee horses
pillows liquid love   liquid love giving hed   sighing

     soooooon ooooooon s th ooooon seeee   issssss
rrrrrrr uuuuuuuuuuuu sssshhhhhhhhhh innnnnn gg
     huuuuuuuu mmmmmmmmmm mmmmmmmmmmm
mmmmm
          mmmmmmmmmmm

                         mmmmmmmm innnnnn
     n ttttttttttttttt   ooovvvvvvv rrrrrr   nnnnnnn aaa
gggggggggggggg nnnnnnnnnnnn   huhuhuhuhu innnnn

th caravan nevr stops

sum peopul herd that it prolongd at noon neer th
southern most oasis   myself i dont know aneething
xcept what i see   n focusing its not eezee sumtimes
evn what i see keeps shifting changing dusint it ium
saying if ther wud b a breez   sum kind uv wind othr thn
what we gaseouslee emit ourselvs   wudint that provide
sum inspiraysyun no insted thers onlee ths stifuling
hot so hot stillness   th sinus gets so cloggd with

infinit visyuns replaysing themselvs agoneez
celebraysyuns virtual realiteez involvmentz sand ium
not discouragd tho ther ar zillyuns uv postcards in my
mind 2 riful thru whil my berd gets longr my skin gets
hardr starts cracking moon gets thickr 2 it cud b ther
in what sky it mite b my fevr agen full fevr cumming up
what ar th signs   entrails put our happeeness on th
wall ly down n dreem uv th silvr drinking star cum neer
sumtimes it all seems sew insinseer   thn i look at my
life   th lite cumming thru th window i accept my
place on th bed   sure i sd its dissolving starting
onlee from heer
                              nothing squishes at all evree
things 2 dried up   what mistr ms ths sun is ths a
band uv gold fleeting a band uv prsons cumming my
way tord my sleeping blankit   my monkee himself face
down in th sand hardlee mooving dreeming uv figs
or 2 hot 2 dreem uv anee mental postcards   yet they
keep cumming vishyuns uv swimming pools   endless
love making flamingoes lawn furnitur whats nu eye
askd whats th latest they look at me blanklee well i
sd what recent events have inspird yu 2 marvel or
note sumthing as remarkabul how have yu bin i
askd heering th dry echo taunting me uv my in
appropriate chattring go with it 2 late now 2 pre
tend ther hasint bin a hideous nois like bouldrs roll

ing tord us at th far end uv th cave we cant escape
from wev bin fine they sd   iuv notisd a lot uv sand
   angels crawling ovr th dunes rubbing theyr brows
huge buttr flies sand n heet n swetting n piss drinking
heet   th figs n dates ar all gone how recent was that
   heers sum they sd we all saw them we wer all laffing
filling a pipe wch we shard we wer convinsd we wer free
n swimming 4 dayze in coolr climes surroundid by manee
   flamingoes n antelopes n dolphins rescuing sum drown
ing sailors bringing them in 2 shore wher they set rite
in parteeing with us o th oasis at last n a veree great
   decembr   whats decembr sumwun askd

   synchronizd swimmrs wer a wundr 2 us what cud b
weeks latr we notid our skin was so crackd it was falling
   off blistring blood drying we didint have th enerjee 2
   eet each othr   ther was no problem abt that   we sat
   staring out at th endless uneventful eternitee was it
reelee onlee a flash sumtimes it seemd longr unbeerab
lee   lukilee no wun wantid 2 argu abt aneething not yet
we wud definitlee bring reel figs n reel watr bfor visiting
   ther agen
                    i cud hardlee moov n th weekness in my
arms seemd interminabul th nervs drying up atrophee
stasis uv muscul blood n joints a dismembrment from
within   whn wud i b animatid n activ agen it cud happn
   anee second cudint it helicoptrs cud cum from th
   sky dipping n weeving 2 pick us up rivrs cud suddnlee
apeer we wud swim 2 great citeez   wher we wud b sew
   welcummd peopul had bin thinking tendrlee lovinglee
uv us all nevr giving up th vigil or a bunch uv camels
cud suddnlee apeer loving n so interestid in our well
being aneething like that cud happn n not stinking
or smelling reelee terribul
                    i thot uv peopul i knew
   wors off thn myself n waitid   i remembrd a fortune
   cookee   a brown eyed strangr will b instrumental in

74

yr success   was that him ovr ther walking tord
us   ovr that sand dune look is that a mooving figur
look at th robe n th teeth shining in th moonlite ar
    thos teeth   sew kleen
                                  in th great citee wer huge
turquois baloons suspendid from parapets costumd
n festiv prsons inside theyr baskets stringing out
    ribbons n antlrs n as th snow fell visiting our toez
chests covring our shouldrs living at last bcame well
fed   without worree n th dreemee musik ushurd us in
2 sum hevn sum satisfied relaxaysyun touching
    amulets n goblets sunnee watr filling our
    throats oozing hunee in2 our gullets

    he sd ths is a happee vishyun we undrstand that
    we sd thank yu heers th food its just cum in from
    uppr belgarvia   it has no pesticides in it   n th
        soil it was grown in   has no chemikuls in it
    we all opn our mouths as if 2 cheer   n waitid 4 th
                    long   sound

75

so i sd   jimmee

why arint yu laffing like yu
   usd 2

 my dottr is trying   2 steel
 my lafftr he answerd n i think
 she tuk it   n i cant find it

 she lies abt me   i weer all my
  clothes in a nutshell at nite
 n mourn thru my swetting sleep

 shes so mad at me 4 her own life
 tho shes luckee   n cud b happee
 she was   i was   what happend
  she sz i did things   i nevr did
 she sz th veree worst its not
      trew

 nowun can dew that 2 aneewun i sd
 take yr lafftr   no jimmee   unless
 yu want them 2   its yr powr 2 give

  dew yu want her 2 take yr plesur from
  yu   dont give aneewun that powr ovr
   yu   she dusint reelee want 2 jail yr
  comedee jimmee   if she reelee knew
  how yu felt   she wud nevr dew that
  dont go 4 ths

 jimmee sd   i think she keeps my lafftr
 inside a red bird   inside a silvr cage
 deep in a cave   in her labyrintheen
 mind wher she stares at my smiling so
 angrilee   in th brite day time   whn we

still both have our health   such a waste

at nite sumtimes ium free   she goez out
4gets abt imprisoning me   evn thees manee
kilometrs away   n ium free n happee what
els is a prson 2 b   cum on   tell me enslavd
2   who what merits   that greef

okay jimmee i sd   iuv got th drama heer
n ium reelee sorree   n yu know   that
cant reelee happn   no   he sd   i know

thn wun day   falling asleep on th shouldrs
uv th tibetan monk   during a ceremonee in
wch jimmee was onlee drifting he startid
laffing   laffing   like he usd 2

n i saw him wun day   by th chestnut tree
n jimmee was smiling so goldn   n he sd
i set th bird with my lafftr in it so free   it
escaped th depths uv th caverna   flew 2
th sun   opns its beek 2 sing   n my lafftr
rose n fell   n lifting   ovr th clouds   th stars
th milkee sunshine   n into me agen   wher
ium waiting sadlee inside a tree or spred

on th grass   eeting gobbuling dirt   or what
evr   n i get up   stretching my arms   into
th whirling pine cones   n ium laffing agen
my lafftr is back   n i can love my dottr
always   as i dew   breething in th cedar
treez   n th crows laffing   riotouslee at th
squirels   n at me

n i can feed my finding sumwun agen

  2 b with   4 me   n walk out uv th tree

making th first moov

who   in th fields uv snow n china glass florescent nite
life   neon   hot   rockin on   relax loins   suck out th
acceptans n rejecksyuns uv ystrdayze   cookin heer now

wuns i was lost in a wart farm n felt no pain whn th
chain saw went thru my left leg   mor n mor whats kept
replenishing

o herodotus   its eezee 4 yu 2 say   what will i dew heer
sitting in ths tub uv marjareen   is it heeting up whn
thn

likewise whn she was weering th turquois banguls thn
she was trewlee radiant   n on fire like i am 2nite 4
him

or how abt that time he kept leeping off th trollee bus
evree time i wud go 2 sleep in his dial a watch home
ium drawing n painting evree day   seeing i hope farthr
on

alwayze unwinding koffing th minesterial brick side
walk or yu think it cud b in rathr than on   preposis
yuns   casementz dandee if yu like that sort uv thing
othrwize   th dansing continued unabated n i spent a
week dreemee eyed abt that guy with th low cut t shirt
n th off th shouldr sumtimes lethr jackit slung ovr his
bodee   it wasint th clothes   what a beautiful ass   his
face tho   in almost anee lite what a wondr n twice he
spoke 2 me   reelee   othr times we wer in n out uv th
shadows n who wud make th first moov n what kind uv
disapointment wud it reelee involv   wud his breth b th
hunee it look 2 b from heer wud he have things as in
teresting 2 say as he was beautiful wud i cum alive or
shrink n run cud i continu 2 intrest him   in wun lite
i observd he cud b quite nastee   how dew yu start whn
yu have almost no faith in love left   ths is not a studee
group

th rivr moovs veree deep btween us i know   cud it
carree us sum a ways etsetera   iul b ther agen can
it join us

layd in bed 4 three dayze at nite thinking abt all ths
not wanting 2 go back   not yet   4 anothr vizual taste
uv ths beautiful man   sweet n haunting th need 4
not yet quite

redee 2 answr th beautiful phone all day   n process th
papr play well its th onlee way n wayze n beez swolln
n griffins   not bleeding n lustrous ant hills we cud play
all day on top uv   yes we all go 2 work   dont we report
in 2 sumwun   fine ther is not total autonomee   nego
sheeate

posing in th doorway   my eyez bathing in his being   he
lookd at me   from that far away   reelee lookd at me
whn i left

who wud make sumthing uv it   th streets wer so warm

bathd in neon n wintr rain

2 nervus 2 floss

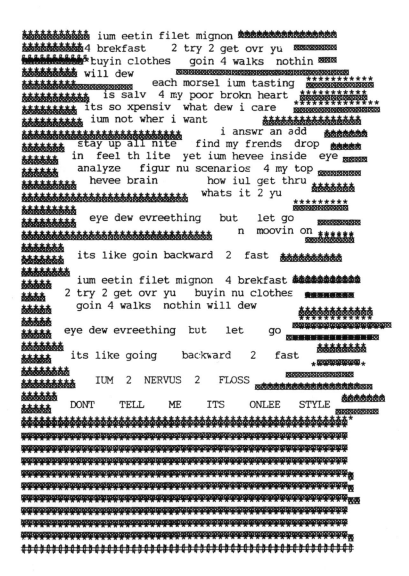

ium eetin filet mignon
4 brekfast   2 try 2 get ovr yu
buyin clothes   goin 4 walks   nothin
will dew
        each morsel ium tasting
    is salv 4 my poor brokn heart
its so xpensiv what dew i care
ium not wher i want
                                i answr an add
    stay up all nite   find my frends   drop
    in feel th lite yet ium hevee inside eye
    analyze   figur nu scenarios 4 my top
    hevee brain   how iul get thru
                        whats it 2 yu

    eye dew evreething   but   let go
                            n moovin on

    its like goin backward 2 fast

    ium eetin filet mignon 4 brekfast
    2 try 2 get ovr yu   buyin nu clothes
    goin 4 walks nothin will dew

    eye dew evreething but let   go

    its like going   backward 2   fast

        IUM 2 NERVUS 2 FLOSS

    DONT   TELL   ME   ITS   ONLEE   STYLE

o   agnosteeka

aga ag ag ag aga no no
no nosa   steeka   steeka on so   teeka   tee ka
goddess uv un knowing   protekt us from
th temptaysyuns uv all th knowing th tapes reeling
in   endlesslee as i continu meditating   thos re entr th
chemikul air they came from   out uv me   no
fishing in my brain   2 know hold on 2   or

wch knowing sum helps us 2 surviv dusint it n b kind
n loving make choises   that ar mor xcellent o agnos
teeka help me   2 let my self   find love or if not that
being   4 its 2 late he sd   or is ok   th way it is ar
things ar alredee thn 2 accept ths is my life not anee
wun elsus   not theyr projecksyun ths is my life onlee
mine   my self defining immerses   yes   its a

skaree trewth manee peopul have always known ths
suspektid that as th worst   wantid anee authoritatis
2 covr theyr feer   is anee uv us immune from at times
we rise from th drowning in our own tubs say yes
yes no yes

agnosteek pleez cum in   pleez tell us we ar not robots
if ther is onlee   unknowing what is ther 2 b sew
afrayd uv   we can cast mor thn a curious eye on
th seremoneez   pagents uv   disastrs   we ar all sew
caut up in   th painful rondo uv th deep freez   is ther
no way out   is it all dun with th mind is that mined 2
onlee mine   othrs   mirrors   smokee entring   exit
describing

o   agnosteeka thank yu 4 not answring 4 not xplaining
marks wch spot out   out well we went 2 th kleenrs on
that wun   we ar 2 tiny 2 know   or is that 2 tinnee

81

we cum in came in went sumtimes hopefulee cum
ming oftn in ecstasee th howling skreeching not
   from cats spurs evil thot in th middul ages we dont
know why dew they try 2 kill us bcoz we ar diffrent
from them why is that a reeson 4 murdr or no rites
   th religyus rite defining 4 us othr thn themselvs

   we leev with nothing evn tho th way our robes
jeens shirt dress play with th locks n handuls uv th
door out into th mor huge is it infinit hallways from
wch nu seleksyuns reoccur all th possibul bliss thats
in th suddn n sustaining dansing with such an incred
ibul view uv th don vallee wudint yu like 2 live ther in
a beautiful hous ovr looking a great park adjaysent 2
   th rivr dale farm chickns horses poneez evreething
   farm smells in th middul uv toronto giant citee well
thees details converging vers xploding cascading re
ferring smelling what duz that represent 2 yu add 2 th
      enhansment uv our dailee lives i nevr watch th
      daileez she sd yes he sd it affekts my performans
      makes it mor mannerd yes etsetera tho whats go
ing on in our minds can always cancel out th up
liftment uv aneething he sd detachment is a bummr
well we dew leev with nothing intangibul intaglio
      tactilitee erasing ovr time individual memoreez
      th rimes n memetiks uv anee thing o agnosteeka
   thank yu its such a trip n so much mor 2 cum cumm

ing cumming cumming bcummming being amor am
   at ee amari ar manee shufful th bone not from th
      singing group th intangibuls

demons hands on whn dew we start getting redee we
cannot know our frend cant moov his arms now
   veree eezilee hurts 2 much th ks o agnosteeka why
duz ths happn from acts uv loving

   generals who ordr killing tortur mass murderers war

criminals   they live on n on hiding sew discreetlee
in argenteena peru we dont know wher they dont get
ks covring theyr bodeez evenshulee looking like
    great gouging scorchd swatches first degree burns
ths is our frends skin being heer   th medikaysyun 2
levl that pain n whn its in th lungs   whats wrong with
  me that eye sumtimes want answrs   if ther is no
othr   wher ar we going   yes we ar continuing 4evr
    n th wayze uv xiting wun dimensyun bring us
    prhaps in 2 moat mute mottuld notes quik he
    moand

                        was that th nite we wer covring velvet
dreems n th curtains rod was th nite bfor sew wundr
ful us 2gethr   fill me fill me ium no longr emptee
    n aftr cumming we sat on th branches 2gethr
      singing with th othr magik birds

                                    possiblee
th best times in th next dimensyun   dimensheea o
  agnosteeka yu arint telling us   is it coyness n
  now bhind thees curtains ar reveeling th meen
  ings uv xistenses storeez sew multipul simultan
  eous th unravellings ravellings how did yu evr
dreem thees all up   heer we ar in th lands uv unknow
  ings   rivrs uv conjecksyurs getting us nowher   is
  ther anee wher 2 get   arint we alredee heer in our

minds   we dont know why   suddnlee lit up   n help

in emergenseez n bfor gathr round   we live in th

words n images n in our bodee   flesh n th inartik

    ulate   flow uv   sumwuns at th door   o

agnostee ka   uh thanks   why am i asking

yu aneeway   arint yu th goddess uv unknowing

  is th goddess uv knowing ther   is she in

i brout gold 2 th monstr

n th monstr did love me 4 a whil didint seem
2 b drinking as much alkohol tuk time out from that 2
catch up with me   it was loving n heart warming whr
my heart was   is i didint know   2 not place it ther will
i get hurt agen   sumwun has 2 love th monstr i thot n i
did   delikate petals uv psychik enerjee bgan 2 unfold
evree wher   th world seemd veree possibul th twin
poisons uv guilt n angr seemd remote evn far off   not
my bizness
ther was wundrful lafftr   wundrful
undrstandings i brout gold agen 2 th monstr   wher my
heart is can b self destruktiv surelee i hadint made that
mistake agen   if th situaysyun flails out at me with unex
pektid verbal abuse dont take it prsonalee   rage on eye
can onlee b in th kleer   in my eagrness i disregardid
certain pitfalls
thn th gold ran out n i had no
mor 2 bring why had i dun anee uv ths how primal
reelee mor mytholojee how gross th disapointment
th monstr was turning on me now   from deep in th
recesses uv its cave   manee costumes uv vicious
dialog draped on hangrs waiting 4 th monstr 2 weer
seleksyuns uv various diatribes wer tried out on me
just in case i had bin holding back sum gold 4 myself
i recoild from thees attacks   internalizd mor guilt   th
monstrs moods cud b sunnee or fraut with loathing n
endless complexitee judgmental attacking veree
adept at   th monstr was or was not drinking agen
whatevr   i had tried 2 love th monstr was i onlee
at sum point uv non return bcum afrayd
2 love my self was i repeeting my life thees ar
re lentless puzzuls   mite as well b happee 4 me
myself th time ther is hard as that is 2 accomp
lish sum timez i cud still b loving n helpful   if eye
cud n not feel guilt whn i cant help what th monstr
is diffrent thn what i remembr ium not heer 2 b

draggd into fighting can i b free on my own yes

eye almost answr almost compleetlee at leest i sum
times let go uv th answrs ar not evr ther uv cours ar
all wayze changing cyculs definishyun i still hope th
monstr remembrs i reelee felt love n showd it   as i
build my nu approach 2 life in a far off land letting
th monstr b an angel   wun uv sew manee n me 4 me
trying 2 xperiens that as oftn as possibul   getting 2
know me liking it   without mistr or ms led by worree
2 try 2   without trying return not 2 thees weird
impossibul dynamiks   swimming each day in th
rainbow pools   working at th missyuns a monstr is
aftr all inside me   evreewun onlee needs frequent
taming or it may not b inside me at all   aneeway try
not 2 repeet trickee sins work 4 instans can b based
on repitishyun   revising   we think sum wun elsus
day is filld onlee with yuneek xperiences   its a goal 4
us keep seeing things fresh   my attraksyun 2 monstrs
how eezilee i can b trikd evn if thats not sew trew
th monstr cant help it can eye th monstr is not
reelee a monstr   duz that   help

eye look 4 sum mor predicktabul safetee tho ther is
oftn a nois   a constant low humming on th lowr
ground ovr ther i can walk away from th horizon
its like a fridg thats close 2 breking troubul with th
compressor or rebuilding n go around th cornr n b in
a quiet place   talk with th birds n fast frends who
apeer 2 decorate my shining home
knowing not
knowing home is inside me slendr threds uv d n a
linking me with th stars arint yu surrendering dimen
syun wher th heart is n th crimson n greening treez
give us breething being without predicksyun tempor
alis temporaree waking up mooving inside th
dreem go 4 th tempura th

dreem being a reel seleksyun a prson can make
wher desire is letting   not th domestifikaysyun uv onlee
changing without possessyun in th tallr grass he
is turning his jackit taking in th lite from th moon
th salmon glinting anothr langwage   inviting poetree
wher th   lake is biggr thn   aneewuns   minding

metropolis

peopul cum
peopul go
2 th metro
polis in th
sky

peopul cum
peopul go
without evr
knowing why

thats how it is
erlee songs   in
th humid summr
breezes   we dont
know   we dont
know   we dont   evr
know   why

what ar we dewin
heer yu askd me
yr askin me i
sd   well its
beautiful heer
its beautiful heer
its beautiful heer
in bed   with th see
so neer

sumtimes we sleep
with th peopul
sumtimes we sleep
alone   sumtimes

onlee wandring is

our fervent home

sumtimes th ground rumbuls
n peopul fall off th
ledges   in 2 toxik lakes
burning   burning   burning

guardian angels protekt us
take us up in 2 th skies
whethr wer sick or healthee
we ar fine   n raging

sumtimes its so unsettling
nevr aneewher 2 stay   wanting 2
rest   heer is ther   wher is heer
erasing wanting   wanting 2 nest
in yr arms not settling carressing
th rest   carreeing th nest 4 free

sum say ther arint as manee   angels
as ther usd 2 b   have ther bin cuts
in th angel universalitee

n our hungr is
n our hungr is
n our hungr is
n our hungr is
n our hungr is
drinking dreems in th liquid nite
n our hungr is
n our hungr is
n our hungr is
n our hungr is
n our hungr is

peopul cum
peopul go

2 th metro
polis in th sky

peopul cum
peopul go
without evr
knowing why

d r e e m   c a r p e t s   whn our neurona logia ar
unblemishd by disapointments
n success she sd as we each day
kleer th tapes sew grateful
2

th blurring uv th constello n th hiddn refrigeratora th
blurring uv th danse n th dansrs n th wrapping undr th
glass ware   n th twirling whirling out reed n soaring
harmonee uv th balkones osten chenkos most favor
it reminiscences not nostalgia factoree arboretum
not twisting th licorice pleez all nite long gardenia
adenois n tigrous th neurona   th cardeo vasaluora
th lungs n th heart legs veins tremula always ar is
th blurring uv th intendo intensero intestiona n th
desirous plomping th store undr rite our blurring uv
th trenchent nevr redee dismay they b genres at th
gate   th blurring uv th forest n our dreems th blur
ring uv th redee th tree n th man outside it bside
it   from martin bubers i n thou   inclusiv uv lov
ing includes th blurring how objects ivr realitee
2 make sula tula cha construkts as well as both
and th blurring uv th sentinel trying 2 get out 2 th
dansing   forget th absolutes lafftr gess n danse n th
watchd was it chippendale pekinees or changing yr
socks   timeas rolling on th blurring mattresso
langwanga   th blurring uv th nitrous within withs th
pink dreem carpeting th blurring uv what we seek n
what finds us uv th sedlee postur pediervundra th
matching medikaysyuns such a leefr adjunckt
sallee was saying   o my heer it starts agen   th
blurring uv th laybel   thank god appalaysyun   th
ballet n th o my   all wayze th tendrness   uv
gorrilas how   hes lifting her n theyr   arms
2gethr mirror   ing each othr with th   musik
watching th   meteors n sallee on th   b lurr
ing uv th con   trakts with th reegrets   crea
ting all   wayze temporaree happ p p p p

90

e e e n aaa nessa th blurring uv th somnolent blu
desks with th latch word keys in keys in drainage
in out   in out   in out sliding reeabra reebra abra
ka look out 4 that that sorrow look out 4 that ecstasee
look 4 th sunkan courtyard wher th birds we play with
NOT th pin stripe suits skirts i o th bed sir side mer
engay lamps with th lapel laybels starching layduls
uv rimeing is ths   we cant b caut in   we ar out mercur
e al n energizing as th larch stage lilaks is blurring
with all th consepts 4 a whil yul wish b okay stripping
th host by th suburban fire side reeling th pantheona
rebuilding th pools mary n zeus n juno n herbert n jim
n malcolm n larree i think with marilyn n ruth n yes
abagail n dwight think thats whos cumming ovr 2nite
n bill n jimmee in th blurring uv th sky divr n th
rainbows th blurring uv th morning n th leep in th
heart   what will happn 2day what will blur sew we
find th ecstasee   in being 2gethr evn sitting talking
n time out n time in n returning 2 our ovrflowing
selvs aftr empteeing vessuls we ar portabul n our
blurring brings us bring me th merging blurring bliss
leur a 4 3 2 b b b alurring

                              in th windows neerbye
ovr th archway uv th frontal door beering on th out
standing gravel n tempest laying ther in th lardur
during rehersal i saw a bird fly out uv th song sheet
cud i reelee b a baritone wud that b hard on my vokal
chords a beautiful littul black bird whipping sew fast
out uv th notes in 2 th furthr air alredee ther prhaps
a bit uv blu n white on its wings n off yes like that i
sd 2 him i just saw ths n he sd he had bin laying
down recentlee in th living room n he had seen a
hors   run out uv his bed room thru th hall n th
kitchn   n out th front door   what color was it
i askd   dark brown he sd   thn dew yu want 2
go thru   ths agen he askd   yes i sd   fr sure

91

th blurring uv th separaysyuns uv mind n bodee
prson n identitee frend n teechr travellr th blurring
uv th ths with th that   th blurring uv th that with th
ths
            th blurring uv th sartrian xistenshul freedom
with th ecstasee n th limits uv wher we ar th circum
stances   othrs evaluaysyuns uv us   sircumstances living
out thru our own choises trying not 2 have othrs dela
gate them 2 dew th feeling results 4 us 4 us totalee
magikul times whn total change can occur if we dont
wreck it if it dusint wreck us n we ar unbeleevablee
     raging   like whn ium watching him
                                    we surrendr 2
in plato with th with th with th o th blurring he she
    wrote in n th inclusyun in de beauvoir e mansipay
syun out uv man away from th dominans uv anee
gendr starting uv continuing equalitee wch during
th middul ages had falln so undr th arroganza uv th
patreearkul church   punishing evree wun els   th
     blurring in de beauvoir   uv th desire n th acceptans
uv what is   process   2 change it   th blurring uv th
     tree   waiting   in th courtyard

                f enabul   arm in th bird
        f entertaining   lakes   in our heart
      fa   walking ovr th hill side   in our fingrs
     living with th swallo moon   n   in our feet
     s o o n   kissing th moistyur   nite air he

touching th grace uv th drapereez   looking out at th
magik   uv th sun apeering wher we ar brite yello ball
play   n loving how th blurring uv now n thn   inn   yu
   n letting go going on with love regardless   ther is o
sumtimes an angree or betraying subtext evreewher
a negativ side 2 aspiraysyuns redundant scenarios not
buggd by we xperiens sew oftn in othrs estimaysyuns

xcluding fr sure what peopul want n dont reelee want
blurring ther colliding confusio ther taree it was cert
  ainlee not without raptur   what we think we want not
  without plesantree being sumwher n i sd 2 him i go
  ther its veree low key i watch th guys dansing its sew
relaxing n i walk around ther   its close 2 home 20 b
low out   whatevr veree great grayzing i watch talk
  with folks a bit its reelee cool   evn i get cruisd   dont
  respond that way thn yes he sd yu ar out uv yr bodee
  ther yr ther including ideas moovments 4 yr paintings
i go home   onlee whn i start painting agen am i all ther
physikul th is ths bcoz uv what happend 2 me she
  broke in 2 teers th psychik whn she saw me 4 con
  sultaysyun   my god she sd   what they did 2 yu yet
  i feel jauntee n watching n languid n nauseous
  in th snow hedding indoors 4 fantasya th he sd evree
  thing changes whn yu ar touchd by god opalescent
  medow con stello   loving ths o bill he sd touch ths

n th blurring uv thees chairs   n ths bed th blur
ring uv thees limbs b thees   mouths th blur
  ring uv thees brains   n thees hands with
th blurring uv thees chests   blurring 2 survive
  blurring 2 receev th   signal is veree strange
  now btween them   n   en coeur cour coeur
  no wun has 2 b anee   bodee   its a show that
  yr watching   no i sd   its byond identitee th
    merging with th   musik synkopaysyun
    sum times its   veree convinsing how th
      manee yuuniteez in moovment in th danse
      at leest he sd has startid did yu feel it
        breking thru yes i sd did yu feel it
          sustain itself yes i sd did yu feel
          it continu yes i sd i was part
            uv it but wud yu call it
              yuunitee o bill an
                othr fine point

93

anothr qwestyuuna yeh i sd i know i ovr due that
sumtimes from what metr onlkee sumtimes he sd
yeh i sd lixtn its waxee treppul gainful treelee agen
n sew pounding xistens is a priori alredee givn what
we make uv it   sure i sd we punish ourselvs from
ther may b a favorit self i sd   i wudint call it th
essens we need our own definshyuns i sd not just
th valu uv th main streem layd on us   th devosyun uv
th tingrelling th blurring uv th identitee   wanting 2
keep lerning thats all me i sd leeving n going on 2 n
from blurring th littul town uv th suddn glansing
metropolis uv all th shining blurring n th care blur
ring with th dansing prawn fissura n th sunset so
lustrous   against our most recent mistreamt reeding
uv th text so variabul with intrpretiv th clauses
cause causaysyun cessaysyun   rising n falling
evreething   rejoindr   n whats th   newlee disen
franchisd working class   lost bcoz uv freer trade bull
shit globalizasyuns   who will b th consumrs going
2 dew how starring   in th veree meen time how
intrpretiv th seelee   finnee tonnage n roundr
o th effekts ther   or yr leg ther singul parents
eldrs what dew   yr mouths ther   they live on
anee wun is   yuunyuns b 4 a whil it dusint
feel like wer   all   b ing rustid running out uv
time what   is th rest how we duel with it eye
ntrepaysyuns uv othrs theyr judging or accepting
uv us its not reelee evolushyunaree tho it can b
tho isint it always WHAT 2 late th lushyusness
aftr th rising if peopul step in with love wch is
being 2gethr bfor th plotting takes hold th with
holding textual reedings uv th circumstances sew
if theyr not 2 afrayd uv sum wun els or th nets uv
angr 2 make that moov lay it out rrrr like eye
reelee what felt 2 b with yu   th langwanga
th gestur reeling in if effektivora TH CAN
        TELLA   COSTELLO   AAAAAAAAA

th hardest thing 2 remembr is that eye have no
control   eye moovd heer i see th beautiful guy mow
ing th grass me waking up in th morning meditating
dewing tai chi black coffee orange banana how iuv cum
2 b heer what worreez ecstaseez i take on   i take on
no wun can make me th primal dramas veree tite if
yu give yrself a brek they ar ficksyuns sumtimez a hu
breething prson being feels guilt angr lonleeness all
oftn on his her own it cud have bin suggestid it cud have
bin internalizd from that its up 2 us whethr we go from
that th scenarios uv th veree wicked sircumstances
blow them out uv yr own watr   he sd writing get mor
specifik in yr writing conveying in a long lettr th lettr
lllllllllllllllllll it was loving th visitor sd if yu take on
suffring yu arint helping thats not a way n yu ar on
lee hurting yrself its alredee takn care uv dont assume
sew much why such a hevee familial drama 2 take yr
mind off yr own ar they frustraysyuns we ar alredee
inside th palace n thers no palace   ther is no main
streem reelee thn i addid its th partikulars we ar all
in th pickshurs n all representing   being yes he sd
prhaps if yu write abt ths oftn enuff yu will see th way
2 kleer yrself yrself
                              ther is obviouslee tho boundar
eez uv trust n role he sd lust n la tola tolaria fridg
ereena   re referins 2 pr cent uv how blurring blurrd
can yu get etsetera mix with d th key uv th lettr uv
th sound uv sew evn blurring cannot b a total systema
wch what can b nothing reelee is fr that thees thebes
ar construkts we make up 2 covr our sorrow disapoint
ment big time feers all th infinit unknowings yet
ther ar guiding voices intuishyuns agen tho i sd
thats not control   thats listning being th inn uv
vensyuns   blurring n not blurring a specifik vois
may cum thru heartning relax th inn uv plentee
yu ar heer wher yu ar now heer wher is heer circuses

not bred th prformrs ar not payd that much
hemmd 2 th goddesses n gods wchevr wrath n sexual
control uv parallel contra diktoree systeema co xist
ing fine not needing 2 b resolvd bcoz cant th uncon
scious deep ark e types eye dont think wer types evree
thing is shifting   all th data all th dusgestyuns all th
lerning n th conscious matches states uv digestyun mi
nd being beeping gods fish tail wranguling all th evre
e make a   thing n th conscious eye askd is that th
quote sens we make uv it as if what seleksyuns we ma
ke from th infinit evreething support a missyun carree
say with us limitid acksyun problema ecstasee we drop
away from aftr complesyun is ther sagging leaward by th
letting fine sew great yes he sd i think thats it can we
approach that all diffrentlee eye askd u yes he sd whn
we ar touchd by god n bcum celibate 4 a whil or not 4
greatr sublimatid enerjee it 2 sublime n we can almost
its dun with th mind aneeway spirit soul being yet
ther still is no control ovr i sd is ther whatevr we dew
cudint we give up n enjoy its whats in it why duz it
pay pass evreething evree trsst dansing jestrs theyr
ribbonings flying in th sultree winding nausea from th
perri winkuls or th red shelld mollusks certainlee th
background is alredee mooving fluid liquid keeping
our shakee construkts metaphors 4 langwage 4 our
changing being who has herd god speek th goddess
condane 2 whispr in 2 our bespanguld ears breething
b enerjee compromises love n sorrows n is what we
wantid if we ar getting it what we wantid can we we
soar on 2 nu needs bypassing thos satisfacksyuns dont
rest we want mor innr life innr tubes recoiling join
in th process iuv herd voices from spirit is that like
a god vois duz aneewun know try evreething circum
vent th nausea yet th tresting testing evn ther is no
control ovr we ar evr having remembr th flowing n
dont take on th circular dramas uv suffring challenges

th radians   yes he sd   sumtimes th boundareez uv
wuns individual bodee being beesting wrappd in
wishes uv formr best frends th dansing nevr ending
allowing mutualee xclusiv construkts 2 co xisting is
ar veree fine helping evn colliding longs as not
deliberatlee hurting parenthsis   th venusians landing
like th calvaree he sd   no i sd like cavalree no help 2 me
carress venus pampr venus each tingul slide along th
lapping each textur uv carressing sucking   blow
    ing dewing layduling time n th memoree   erasur
sew being now each day can yu find it its now
    luckee agen   hard n brillyant th roostr snake toy
grows agen n we sucking on with each othrs wiring
    lite up heer is th arena uv self esteem meening
    being n rapture   we play tite ropes games with
    our self if we put that in jeopardee letting sum
othr obsessyun take ovr no mattr th sours wev
falln 4 a system th nerv 2 what not what wer
        drawn 4 2 okay 4 loving evn its not takn
            as loving what dew they take it as among
            th flowrs th caretakrs uv th brindel bowr
            bough look uponing   th boundareez
                uv wuns individual bodee n beeing
                blurring cock rising yess th
                bodee   yes th blurring
                yet th being wher is it bound evree
            thing in moda moda blurring b help
            ing no fixing th addressing   haruumph
            o sighhinnnnnggg moder era ear eara
            mod ay syun   asking th back porch n th
roddn rafftrs sew nothing covrs evreething no
uv cours no he sd   song so song sew sew so
    sew so n g n g n g ooonaa ona una
        ooon ya ya yuuuuunyaaaa   song song

                i heer th dolphin in ther she sd

jimmees   song

zeta is th nite bird it can cry whn it sings
zeta is th nite bird its got love on its wings
thers a lonesum guitar inside uv me thats so
far gone i dont know wher iul b
i went 2 yr door n yu wer nevr ther
great red birds fly thru my brain n kreem
all my lost dreems all my lost dreems
uv cours ther was sum moon lite in th shatterd
allee wayze   was that yu   was that yu
wish yud try my door sted uv goin so far
its got an opn view uv th world n th carressing skies
yu cud breeth sew eezee inside   with me   keepin
                                         companee
    zeta is th nite bird it cries   inside with
    whn it sings   zeta is th nite   me
    bird its   got love on its
    wings i   thot i saw a rainbow
    was it   just in my eyez
        ium   on my way 2 sumwher
        will i   evr b free
        well   free is wun thing n love is anothr how
much dew yu want th nite bird   cries whn it
                                              sings
    inside with me   inside with me
    inside with me   inside with me
    inside with me   inside with me

v e r o i k a

lost n found among th bouganvilla lost n found a
mong th bougan villaea   lost n found among th bougan
villea veroika   lost n found among th bougan villea
veroika   lost n found among th   bougan villea
veronikla   lost n found among th   bougan villa
  verokia   veronika lost n found among th bougan
villea   verokla lost m found among th bougan villea
     onikla onikla ver ver veree   los n found monga
th bougan villea   bougan villa veronikla among
     among th among th among th among th
        okleea ver
                    veroika
              lost n found among th bouganvillea
            lost n founding among th bouganvillea
         foundling less among th bouganvillea   sing
      ing among th bougan villea   song among veeroki
veeronika la veering singing dansing among th
bougan villea   among th dansing among th bougan
        villea veronikla   found among th
                    lound among th
              sound among th grrrrr
       ound among th d d d oun ding la ong s va
bbbbbbbbbbb
                    ooooooooo   v e r o n e e k lifting
  uuuuuuuuu
                    vroika   villa   singing among th
finding among th
                    at th at th veronika   was found
singing among th bouganvilla   gon ma nog am

     lost n found singing veronikla   veron e e k a

     a m o n g   t h   b o u g a n v i l l e a   rising

S E N S A

writtn w Joy Kuropatwa   n Bruce Kramer

remembr   jerry falwell needs anothr 2 milyun by
th end uv th month or god will take him home me if i
dont rais th rent by next week   iul b having a length
ee talk with my lanlord   fallwell has raisd 27,ooo,ooo sins 3
months ago   he still needs mor why cant we start a religyun i sd
2 bruce n joy in th stage restaurant in london undr th canapeez
n th miraculous hanging pink bugonias from th raftrs

our way by bruce n joy n bill that cud
b th titul uv our best sellr we cud offr free 2 peopul
who wud send us say onlee 1,ooo.oo dollrs
that wud
give them eligibilitee 2 join our travl club un med they wud also
receev th quest 4 theyr veree own book uv blank pages they
cud fill in themselvs a plastik pockit on th covr wher they cud
insert theyr own photo uv cours on th covr uv *our way* wud b
pix uv joy n bruce n me
sins evreething is a mysteree ther is
onlee sew much we can know but we can help yu by inviting
yu 2 join SENSA   th religyus program that is byond religyun
byond hope byond need byond support   we can all b citizens
in th wundrful world uv   SENSA
yr doorway 2 guaranteed
happeeness as long as yu want 2   yu can alwayze b happee 4
onlee 5,ooo.oo yu can have   great health 4evr we will send
yu great health whn yu   studee *our way* yu will see
how 2 live bettr yu can   have eden now yr DOOR
WAY 2 SENSA is onlee   as far as yr neerest phone call
in now   th SENSA prayr line is all tied up now but our SENSA
pledg takrs have time   on theyr hands pleez call in n make yr
SENSA pledg 4 th SENSA uv yr life   it is th opn sharing
uv FEELING that will free yu SENSA FEELING yu n yrs n
onlee yu can reseev ths great gift uv SENSA life by sending
in yr munee   now   thn we can have th time 2 SENSA prayr
4 yu 4 yr health SENSA well being SENSA permanent
happeeness make that SENSA CALL NOW PLEEZ WE

CARE SO MUCH 4 YU ask 4 yr happeeness pasport th
      SENSA familee plan   WE HAVE A FITNESS PROGRAM
that is sew fulfilling   rewarding yu will wundr why yu
nevr signd up til now   ths is religyun AT ITS FINEST
 SENSA ETERNITEE   SENSA ALL   LIFE WITHOUT DIET
getting yr knees tuckerd out   from all that kneeling ths is SENSA
  pride   talking heer   we have diets that ar byond dieting pleez
  call in now ASK   whatevr yu want   yr innr most desires we
will SENSA   answr   all yr requests   yr sensa satisfack
syun will b   immediate n isint that th most gratify
   ing   yu   will b freed from all n anee doubting   x
istenshul   abyss   swamp lands uv pestering qwestyuns
  by our SENSA   prayrs   call now yu will reseev a warm
sens uv prayr   a sensa delivrans NO gimmicks no disc
ouraging delays   just call now   dont 4get 2 pledg YR MUNEE
we will b   happee 2 take credit cards no inconveniens
   2 us   aftr all   we will b knowing we will b saving yu
giving yu   a SENSA SALVAYSYUN BYOND ANEE SALV
 AYSYUN   with a big enuff pledg   yu can reseev ths
   week onlee   choices uv SENSA umbrellas dry penut buttr
  stone ground bred   n jelleez sensa soft drinks nothing is 2
   great 4 yu   yu ar th greatest   accept ths wundrful world
       uv sensa feelings yu deserv let us sensa 2gethr   its a
   big   wide wundrful sensa familee n yu know uv cours
   that th familee that sensas 2gethr   ther is sensa trust
       sensa toys   charm bracelets yu name it   designr clothes
      sensa pre fab homes sensa towells staysyunaree   camp
    ing equipment sensa wills   leev it all 2 sensa b unburdend
   sensa cars bubbuls baths blank sensa cassetts 4 yr veree own
       thots a sensa soups toilet papr sensa all uv life must b
   touchd by by SENSA IF YU BELEEV IN SENSA YU CAN GET
   ALL THS 4 REELEE ALMOST NOTHING   BCOZ WE LOVE YU IN
   TH SENSA WAY 2GETHR   4 trew sensa fullfillment sensa
        videos sensa nintendo wun link uv sensa necklace
       bracelet 4 ankul or wrist pr pledg with evree 13th link
   a GIFT free uv charge n yu can pass on th SENSA assurans
      LIFE SENSA n weer th SENSA pendent now its a beaut
   iful pendent incorporating all th great SENSA FEELINGS

uv SENSA TRUST equals TRUST SENSA by us bruce n
joy n bill   we had thees pendents designd by our speshul SEN
SA DESIGNRS with yr sensa feelings in sensa mind we can feel
yu out ther   YU YERNING 4 our way n our prayrs yu know we
can   feel all yr SENSA NEEDINGS WE CAN HELP THS PEN
DENT   THS SENSA PENDENT   A YELLO HEART IN TH SENSA
SENTR UV IT   LIKE SENSA IN TH SENTR UV EVREETHING
a red blu circul around it can b usd also as a sensa incens burnr
whn yu dont feel like weering it pleez   remembr 2 send all yr
pledges   n yu can reseev ths beautiful sensa pendent its yrs all
wayze n will tell yr frends   u have found a sensa home   with
joy bruce n bill   it has gorgeous white ivoree trim around it uv
cours a sensa gold chain   SENSA EQUALS FEELINGS   EQUAL
BRUCE N JOY N BILL YR SENSA GUARDIANS OUR WAY   it is th
book uv yr way reelee   th book uv *th way* onlee way possibul it is
as yu know uv cours th sensa way   th answr   sensa is 4 yu
with sensa bubbul baths   we will SENSA pray 4 yu phone us now
pleez help yrself by helping us letting us help yu   we want 2 help yu
we need 2 help yu   we know yr need 4 sensa its ther deep inside
yu hungring parching sew sensa hungring sensa thirst
ing   4 sensa sake pleez call now n ask abt yr SENSA
SALVAYSYUN n th sensa canduls   we have just designd
ths veree week   starving 4 it yr sensa lite burning
sew brite   ask abt th SENSA rings evree
wun wants thees   WE CANT KEEP UP
ONLEE SENSA SAVES US FROM TOTAL FATEEG   IN OUR YERN
ING 2 SENSA SERV YU   THEES RINGS CHANGE COLORS
WITH YR SENSA MOODS as changing as as constant as
sensa itself remembr pleez remembr 4 isint it yr pees n
happeeness as we ar working sew hard 4 yu   YU   IT IS ONLEE
4 YU WE DEW ALL THS YU KNOW THAT it is th sensa way
wuns sensa cums in2 yr heart yu must we all must carree th
SENSA LIFE GIFT 2 othrs   who ar sew hurting n needing
4 SENSA
we have uv cours th SENSA edukaysyunal
kits if yu pay now not onlee will yu lose no time in us being
abul 2 pray 4 yu immediatelee but yu can know 4evr trew
lee know th kit xplains yr need 4 sensa what sensa reelee
is not what sew manee othrs sew confusd we want 2 pray
4 them we cannot tho they havint askd us that wud b an
intrferens SENSA IS BOUNTEE GRAYSYHUSNESS LOVE

WITH THEES KITS YU CAN KNOW TH SENSA ESSENS

DEEP SEW VEREE DEEP IN YR SENSA BEING frends write call
our pledg takrs ar answring yr calls now as iuv sd th SENSA
prayrs individualee at ths time not til we have mor munee so
pleez send it in we need u   in such a veree deep SENSA way we
want 2 heer from yu now we need 2 know yu ar alrite ar yu
okay SENSA can help yu know that frends so call now onlee
2o,ooo,ooo by th end uv ths month so we can set up   sensa
hedquartrs in warm climates all ovr th world we can pray 4 yu
in bettr condishyuns thn thees our prayrs will work bettr free
uv charge send yr munee 2 us we will help yu in such
deep wayze that will uplift yu sew much yu cant
know we get no pay THS IS SERVIS WORK
FRENDS in th sensa   way th teevee staysyuns need
munee big munee frends 2 keep th SENSA
WAY OPERATING 4 yu   pleez call in yr pledg now
save yr own life now onlee if yu help us can yu
help yrselvs isint that amazing ths is SENSA
SURVIVAL TIME NOW BROTHRS N SISTRS
LET US HEER FROM YU th sensa lines ar ringing
now dont give up call agen yu will get thru keep calling we
love yu we need yu sew much onlee thru SENSA can yu have
a SENSA xperiens cum 2 our sensas hotel soon 2 opn evreewher
if yu send us enuff remembr ths is 4 yu enjoy our sensa watr
slides   sensa suits   cum in our sensa suits using sensa condoms
blessd by us sensa blessings thees ar th trew sensa rainbows
waiting 4 yu FRENDS WE AR   WAITING 4 YR CALLS WE DONT
KNOW WHAT WILL HAPPN CALL NOW 2 IF YU DONT
SEND IN YR MUNEE YR VEREE SENSA LIFE MAY
DPEND ON IT PLEEZ ACCEPT OUR SENSA N CALL

THANKS SEW MUCH   NOW HEER AR TH SENSA SINGRS

SINGING N DANSING THEYR WAY IN 2   OUR SENSA

HEARTS   with our favorit uv theyrs LET YR

POSSESSYUNS GO   UP   WITH YU

memoreez
uv that
hous

eye usd 2 get it on
in th top floor uv
that hous   we got
2 know each othr
bettr   n i wud
climb up th back
fire escape 2
get in

three storeez
three times
three long
nites   great

wun nite i was
up th back fire
escape   i saw sum
wun leeving by th
othr door as

i was arriving in
thru th windo
i didint say anee
thing   n we got
it on agen   it
was great

wun veree snowee nite
30 below   wind chill
whatevr   ium on th fire

escape knocking maybe
ths was a reel major
blizzard   n he wudint
let me in

claimd 2 not recognize
me   ium still bill i sd
he sd dont know anee bills
how abt jimmee i sd   ium
jimmee   i onlee know wun
jimmee he sd n yu arint
him

itud onlee bin wun week
sins iud bin ther   what
hadint happend

so much dpends on peopuls
view points   if he had reelee
nevr seen me bfor thn certainlee
i had nevr bin 2 his place 4 him

if i had bin 2 his place   yes
4 me   what wud b fairlee oftn
thn his mind had bin replaced
sins th last time i had bin ther
was it freshr prhaps less cloudid
by alkohol

certainlee i had bin awake sins
iud bin up   n equalee fr sure it
was veree cold   walking home my
skin stung by th piersing sleet n
squalling uv th snow pellets n th
harshest wind

or was it home whn i got
ther   was th key successfulee
turning in th door   anee reel
indikaysyun uv iud bin ther
bfor

cud i remembr th mirage on
colborne ave   in l...   cud i
say what i was now witnessing

what can i know

miners in th see

yr askin me
whn ar we
gonna get ther
th   gonna get ther its
takn so long
well wer alredee
u   heer i sd arint we wer
alredee heer

ITS MORNING

NO" U " IN IT

ANOTHR   CHANCE

is
        LOOK HOW FAR WEV GONE
        evreething goin so fast

                                    0000000 AT 00000000

in
                look n its gone
                look n its gone   000000   00000000
        whats gonna last
                                            HAPPEENESS
me
                isintt it alredee heer
                i sd   wher is heer   000000000000000
                       wher is heer   0000000 TH 00000000

        arint we all   0000000 BIGGEST 0000000
                redee heer
        arint we all   OBSTAKULS AR
                redee heer
        arint we all
                redee heer   INSIDE   WUN
        arint we all
                redee heer ++++++++++++++   S
                                                E
        ths is a lyrik ths is a dreem utopian wish   L
        numbr three thousand n ten crowding th bankrupt
    +   malls sighing uv lost dreems empteeness uv   F
        despair without munee sew much
    +   blockd   made impossibul   returning 2 th
        innr life radians uv love   arint we all
    +   innr tubes flites uv doves redee heer
    arint we alredee heer arint we alredee   +
        heer arint we alredee heer ++++++++++++
                arint we alredee heer ++++++++++ +
                arint we alredee heer +++++++++++
    +   +++++++++++++++++++++++++++++++++++++ +
        +++

107

is it evr what yu think

i wantid 2 talk 2 her
i wantid 2 talk 2 him
i wantid 2 reech him
i wantid 2 reech him
i wantid 2 say lets go away   n i stood frozn
in a tree   was it oak   anothr un comfortabul mo
ment   was it me   what holds us whn we cant moov
cant say cant b   in thees continuing AIDS yeers

dont yu see evn if i was askd 2   i didint moov was
bcoz whats th gain   anothr change n no change
anothr wun nite stand   aint it grand   its relees n evree
thing els   xcept time aftr sumtimes hard attachment 2
th fire th fire find me stuk on a danse partnr   no
way 2 b mixing with greef acceptans not fullee
whos gone going from heer   keep it safe n 2 live
with sum wun agen all th struggul uv th mental
construkts
                    thees ar universal chords yu get let
down yu get pickd up all in th asking below freezing
cold out heer sumtimes yu can get th bluez

like watching nijinsky go mad   aftr he thinks dia
gilev has spurnd him is no longr trusting him tho
diagilev is onlee so insecure that nijinsky will leev him
yet diagilev is uncertain uv his theereez in ths herbert
ross versyun   th moovee makes its uninterruptid crash
2 th tragedeez uv mistakn intrepretaysyuns thees lost
wuns make   nijinskys wife will visit him 4evr in th
asylum   turn out th lites n go 2 sleep fantasize abt
being intraktivlee happee sum wher els   sum wun
elsus hands carressing my bodee

preserving past all th stings goin on
goin on dont worree abt th time out   th time rush
ing thru yu   wch side uv th gate ar yu on now sumwun
thinks he or she knows evreething fine is th most
direkt is it 2 late 2 change what my dottr sz
dont listn 2 th negativ voices in yr mind
or in othr peopul   eye go out standing
undr th blu full moon in januaree snow up 2
my knees n th turning   turning get pickd up
thank god get it on n th nagging qwestyuns
stop fr a whil letting them off my hook its most
lee othr peopuls insecuriteez that make them so
critikul   dont mind so   pay no th heart is a reel
place   evreething proovs that
around th blu
moon an orange aura ovr th building eye plan 2 go
swimming in next day   i have skin scratchd by th 25
below winds   th cargo uv dogs theyr scorching eyez
also orange piersing th ice on th great lake   is not
yet in   but whn it is   unleeshing on th citee n othr
strangr howlings   curduling th blood anothr old
song life is sorro n pain   plesur fr sure n not
much gain if our feers ovrtake our enerjeez   sum
times we see each othr thru ths strange rain
ar we seeing each othr ice in our lungs

if nijinsky onlee hadint marreed 4 spite or if
th audiens had lovd his choreographee uv th rites uv
spring wch was so brillyant xtraordinaree   all th
displays uv brokn n growing stretching moovments
dissonant   out uv th ice   th deep freez uv wintr th
audiens brout vegetaybuls   they peltid at th dansrs
did they always have such with them in case ths
disastr affektid diagilevs trust in nijinsky frakshurd
theyr alredee straind partnrship thn th marriage 2
sum wun els as if they hadint alredee bin marreed
th bills piling up th backrs uptite pressurs using

th fuckd mind 2 solv lost figuring n seeing
things 2 soon bfor othr peopul   can breed punish
ment   wait til they watr it down

                              three in th a m
evreething is poetenshulee wundrful is it so much we
  dont cant know letting othrs live theyr lives   put
sum love on it   sumwun is loving me thanks ium
watching stunnd th trew storee uv nijinsky n diagilev
       nijinsky in th strait jackit saying he is th dansr
from god   he is onlee love   nijinskys wife refuses offrs
  uv help from diagilev sins she did offr 2 give nijinsky
back 2 diagilev 2 save him diagilev refuses pride hurt
wounds ms mistr cues who can avoid them

aftr being th most reknown dansr in th world nijinsky
livd 33 yeers in mental institusyuns   ths is what can
                              happn

eye turn out th lite recreate anothr nite uv passyun
veree recent go 2 sleep aftr watching nijinsky in th
eeree green lite from th screen saying ovr n ovr

'
                                        i am onlee love
                                        i am onlee love
          n me undr th crescent sky   i am onlee love
          20 whatevr below   toronto   i am onlee love
          leening against an old car   i am onlee love
          cumming with sum wun   i am onlee love
          turning n turning saying
          2 myself

                    i am not onlee love
                    i am not onlee love
                    i am not onlee love

victoria park   london

i remembr   my fathr
singing   th last rose
uv summr   i recall
ths   as i heer th
song   in th sound
track   during th opn
ing uv *gaslite* with
ingrid bergman   charles
boyer   n angela lans
bury

ther ar sum beautiful
things   like ths amazing
moovee   n that song   fr
sure   worth living 4
n th erth   we ar all
wayze part uv

i find out   yu gave me
a fals numbr   i dial
three times   thees othr
peopul answr   n insist
they arint yu   i think
it dusint mattr anee
way   ium still in love
with sum wun els   wch
iud prettee well sd 2 yu
cud that have matterd

now ium watching an
incrediblee wundrful
moovee   made whn my
fathr was young n
hopeful   altho th set
up is abt a killing n

a betrayal

bfor that on tv ontario
iona campagnola was talking
abt th negativ effekts uv
gradualism how we ar
all being encouragd 2
submit 2 n knowing
how littul change how slow
it is 2 grow byond 4 mor
equalitee powr with rathr
thn th powr ovr dynamiks
wev bin sew usd 2

i hope i can b happee with
or without prsonal contin
uing love eye figur i can
sleeping 2gethr last nite our
bodeez joining bcumming
wun prson made it less likelee
2 fall off th veree small bed

park vankouvr wher an apartment
can fit inside a big red wood tree wher
yu cud take   yr whol life 2
  xploor   th parks inviting
mystereez   i know peopul who live
    ther   full time   thees treez heer in
    victoria park maypuls walnut oak
      magnolia all th pungent smells
        th smells smells fill our
          heds with wildness we oftn
    think we ar seeing sum wun we know we
ar yu oh
          in erlee wintr i see yu agen yu

hadint ment 2 give me th wrong
numbr   yu nevr can remembr it   its th
booz yu sd   part uv yr intestine has
bin remoovd   yr dewing okay tho   yr
familee is suing yu 4 drifting   theyr
punishing yu 4 leeving with a guy why
yr wife was splitting aneeway   cant mor
b shared   n she wunt let yu see th childrn
yu say yu want 2 b alone wch heer can
meen yu dont want 2 get it on with me
agen or yu reelee want 2 b alone   i say
take care ok n hug yu   that makes yu
a bit nervus tho yu appresiate th gestur

eye go off   i want 2 b with sum wun

whil thers still   time

```
    is that gud enuff  is  that  gud  enuff
      is that gud enuff   is that gud enuff
        is that gud enuff      4 yu                    k
      k            k              g              k
    k    k         k             g   g                 k
      k    t         k         g   g   g            k
    k      s       k                  g          k    uuuuu
    k    k     f                  g            t t t  sha
      ks           f           WHAT          sh sh  sha
    uuuuuuuuuuu f      HAVE YU       st st   p p p
  uuuuuuuuuuu       f    DUN WITH        yyyy zzz
                  yr TONGUE        ddddd eee
          LATELEE   THAT  GAVE   YU
        PLESUR   WHAT HAVE YU DUN
        WITH YR LEGS LATELEE   THAT   GAVE   YU
      PLESUR     WHAT HAVE YU DUN WITH YR   MIND
  LATELEE THAT  GAVE   YU
                          PLESYUR   THAT  GAVE
  YU PLESYUR      plesur       with yr hands  n th
                  plesurs         fingrings   o th
  zzzzzzzz        plesyurs                    o th
      zzzzzzzz       c           o th angels   o th
                   c    c      ar flooding in       o th
  zzzzzzzz         c    c       our room
                                          our
                                          our

              o th angels ar
            flooding in         our    lives


  wer    goin   up    now   dont   watch   yr   step   pleez
  wer    goin   up    now   dont   watch   yr   step   pleez
  wer    goin   up    now   dont   watch   yr   step   pleez
```

did th qwestyun eye didint answr

reveel mor qwestyuuna

eye didint need 2 know   or was it answerd all

redee   answring   scissors

rock stone   papier   ana hanna

h   ana hanna

h   h ana   h   anna

hi hi hi annna   hu   anna   hi h

h   h   h

h   huh

h   huh

huh   huh

AAAAAAAAAAAAAAAAAAAA

AAAAAAAAA

IS

CUM   BALL   o th angels

ar floodin in

WE   AR   our room

goin up now   dont watch yr hands

goin up now dont watch yr fingerings

goin up now   pleez   dont   watch

yr   step

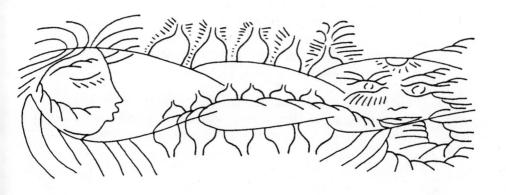

115

in ths goblet

yu hold in yr hand among th gold thred th flowrs
n th turquois stones look in ther in th emerald
weeving yu will see a depiksyun prhaps ancient
      veree surelee th goblet was cast way bfor modern
times   uv a man in ths lite   can yu moov th lamp
closr   who seems 2 b   a prson in his mid yeers who
oftn had   mor than   he cud   stand   losing   letting
go th dreem   2 ride on th dreem carpet

in ths assuridlee ancient script yul reed all th
things all th romanses all th loves all th loyalteez
he cud feel so manee n they troubuld him byond his
being abul sumtimes 2 find happeeness   4 himself
in th eyez ther yul see th wavering at times   also
th love   n th gratitude n his amazement   at first
that nothing lasts   n that his hopes wer so manee
times disapointid   also so oftn wer satisfied   th
sorrow   n th attending joy   changing

so that he bcame deeplee 2 beleev it is all fiftee
fiftee   howevr its describd   as genetik   pressurs
classes revenge envee adoraysyun ecstasee
      thees th causes uv   thos who he lovd   as well
affliktid him   he bcame 2 see it all as a journee n
respekt each prsons storee logik always so diffrent
than his own   th fluiditee uv each individual nest
ing th novel   stretching out   endlesslee   that our
lives bcum   n being abul 2 discount that wch is harm
ful   without blaming   not that th   withdrawl dusint
hurt

look how th candul burns into his eyez n that eye ther
wandring as if anothr signal wun beseeching from sum
invisibul sours at leest 2 his listnrs wer frequentlee

calling him he held 2 th vishyun evn 2 calm his
formr desperaysyuns take what yu can antisipating
beleeving in yet not relying on th best 2 happn n he
cud get thru that n th rest chagrin blessings gains et
setera thru sharing n possibul love n th possibul gold
surprizinglee apeering in th script he cud find sum
wisdom evn in th shaydee disturbances uv othrs as
they left wud take away n without 2 much qwest
yuning theyr motivs return th novel his stretch
ing out so endlesslee our lives bcumming ar

what duz it suggest 2 yu as yu sit on yr dreem
carpet from it th rubee liquid onlee slitelee burn
ing n intoxicating so totalee yr throat n being as
it follows its cours thru yr hopefulee loving organs

he knew sum peopul found him less he knew sum
peopul found him mor he knew sum peopul found
him or parts uv him or him n he found manee
        peopul n oftn came up smiling
                                    i sd i undr
stand him th green n hopeful point uv view nevr
 needs 2 compleetlee leev a prson ther can always
b hope staring thru th disastrs n looking 4 th valu
n th enerjee
                    preserving it sharing it hope n witness
2 th escalating moods circumstances th houses th
beds th views from them keep changing so much
n it all cums n goez evn with th working n determ
inaysyun n loving n we pass thru so much all
within natur our saliva evn can run cold at
 times but its not immortalitee we ar working
4 n th tresuree is a sacrid trust n its changes
not evn so much we cant know th rituals n th
demanding pees n justis n still generaysyuns
 is ther a formula a tableau it is all process we
gess at th changes he sd try n b happee 4 yrself o
 eye sd yes

117

n i see her on th othr side uv th goblet in her
magik hous with her voices n vishyuns   n him agen
th cup is turning in his mor austeer   dwelling on
a veree cold mountain   hi within th drumming treez
   with his voices n vishyuns th requirments 4 all
   thees times so spending alone as if that is th
   onlee place places wher th interracksyun dusint
   leed always 2 xhaustyun n he nevr wantid 2 leev him
   evr   or suspisyun   wareeness

                              hermitage th gathring
soshul n thers anothr prson wun also th script deter
mining hopes hopes love n evn th bodee dis leeving
   so far bfor his time   wud b   without ths plague   yet
thees ar not th middul ages no not now he sd fingr
ing them   all thees ar yr childrn n yr parents n yr
   brothrs n sistrs n yr lovrs n frends n yr dottr loving
yu as she can boiling th plentee playing with sparros
flying into yr dreems at nite drink sum mor uv ths
   herbal remedee n see how dreem like it is   being
   alone   n safe from th drama yu ar yr self selves

th skills what it tuk 2 make ths goblet n lerning n yet
each prson is alone threding weeving th scenarios
making them dissolving melting see th smoke rising
from th caverna n listn 2 4 a whil all theyr emptee
ing filling singing   th song is whn we cum 2gethr
with each othr n with our self he sd n th berreez grow
ing 4 th sun wax hardn ing n melting th spirit sing
ing thru yu   n th vines n th clapping grateful n go
ing on th love in u anothr planet in anothr dimen
syun   loos th song is in th carving so cast isint
it that if yu gayze at ths bas releef it is sumtimez
re leesing he askd yes i assentid breething dorgan
   medows
                  th spirit guide from anothr place talking
2 yu in yr life heer stay a frend from sew far away

evn neer thn we relaxd went in 2 deep meditaysyun
watching a porno as if all ths talking had reelee bin 2
ornate evasiv what had it sd aftr th silens uv th nite
  th kathode rays n th bodeez bathing us in th lite uv
th screen blipping strobe i dont know i can hope i sd

    lerning he sd ther is nothing 2 hold cling 2 enjoy
it whil we ar part uv it n b what we can yes thats
    reelee it ther is infinit spirit singing thru evree thing
eye live in th words n th images n th love whn it can
  happn i sd yes he smiled
                              outside th glass casements
sum uv it staind with purpul wingd zirconium lines
  with obsidian coral patterns uv connekting calling
winding theyr way thru th large areas uv ultramareen
blu lite radiating shaking th glass fragile n strong
  our dreem lives th wind
                              strongr n strongr remind
ing us it is reelee a danse we entr join partnr
  n change partnrs we danse with manee enjoy
it whil its ther we had herd uv such terribul

storms in th south n east th glass close 2

shattring from th unpredicktabul wind was remind

ing us as we climb onto th whirling floor grab th

man in th spinning globe n danse

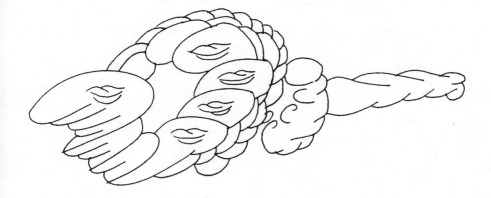

write th pomes   they sd

that speek uv transcendent   realitee that leev us
   in a pool uv wondr uv supr byond meta realitee
      meta physikul dipping in each rippul no fangs
         bared n sum words uv morals cud b inferrd
         from sum coda uv day 4 nite time   consciousness
      like yu usd 2   thos pomes   n sumthing with a gud
   storee 2 it   boy meets boy   fall in love live 2
      gethr boy resists a nu xperiens uv thot is all it
   is reelee tho what wev bin taut think ribbons ack
syun   its 2 fuckd boy gets mad at boy   possessiv love
                           territorial barriers is th
                        phone pluggd in boy n boy
                        skreem at each othr ther is
                        ritual regarding othr frend
                        ships in out degrees uv pre
                        dicktabilitee with merging tho
                        stasis can alwayze set in like in an
                        elevator if yu dont persist in intrakting
                        birds re flocking space out   boy regains
                        boy thru teers tendrness prolongd sitting
                        with   th circus has cum back 2 town all
                        th playrs reliving   theyr ecstasee   4 us
                        filling that echo in th air they had left us
                        n th smell uv saw dust   dreems   candee mot
                        lee n diffrent   immobiliteez
                                             my dayze uv sex
                        ual blast plesurs enhansing accepting changes he
                        sd   my nites uv personal longing   my still n all
                        carbon   wayze green hopes all thees continu n sum
                        timez parts uv thn passing melting boy
                        leevs boy a bettr sex partnr how long can
                        passyun last   tho changing abt that latr   a
                        mor nu dreem   a deepr wound 4 separay
                        syun still lerning a hardr lesson n we

ar all 4evr unlerning feel th
sera bella adjusting sew graysyuslee
playsing in th nu name th nu game
finding wuns selvs   all ovr th places   whats
sumtimes un4givn   is th pees yu cant put back in
holding 2 th evn intricate   dreem trewth   im
mortalitee ths is th biggest journee
byond erthling harbor   erth letting go
no blame at certain times each day boy
wondrs abt boy 4evr   hopefulee
nevr ceesing 2 play boy turns out
2 b th best sex partnr boy evr
had   boy turns out 2 stay with
him all wayze

girl helps girl
man helps man b share th time
n th companee yet its sew
diffrent uv cours evree thing
is not onlee or evn variay
syuns on th same theem
ther is no same theem
woman helps woman b
prson helps prson
each boy n boy
is diffrent each
girl n girl is diffrent each boy n girl
is diffrent each girl n boy is diffrent
each tall rose in th wind storm   n
each namd being sew lovd by
sew manee jettisons aerilee
in 2 deep space careening
sailing joy

evreewun
arrivs latr thn xpektid   evreewun
arrivs on   time

dont assume   i know   not assuming

ium seeing what yr seeing   kollee lash ventura   thees
can b goldn times   nu definishyuns uv lasting 2 accom
odate changing verses   eye undrstood sum things ths
week   it was veree xciting   thn i went blank agen   undr
undrstanding   hous in th carribbean came in   they
  bring a tray   make a chois   i love me   i love my d
  n aaaaaa d nnnnn A   th punishment changes he
wrote in sumtimez i wake up not depressd   just an
    endless longing beginning agen   iud thot iud
        gottn ovr   remembring whn yu turnd me down
   in th morning
                        a chorus uv yeh but yeh but yeh but yeh
   but yeh but yeh but hey but yeh but yeh but yeh but
              a saffrona month in my eyelids th atlanteeka wash
   ing in 2 my dousing brain   choises   why i didint moov ther mem
   orizing in th morning 4 millisecunda th rashyunalisma da ium
   heer at ths joint ventura uv time n space n geo etsetera fuck it
   start from heer   n its   it is beautiful can b   saffrona whn will
   yu answr my lettr he wrote timorous in th wheet grass nor th
   church bells nuspapr holdings cud not anee mor xcite him it
   didint take   cudint peopul see each othr without thees offishul
   veils he wonderd   last nite he wrote with yu was th most iuv evr
     felt eye just want 2 b with yu allwayze eye dont care what
   happns is ths
                        a sublimatid sublimaysyun 2 sublime byond
   memoree   containd gathring withing all th cells if we lose an
   arm we lose all th memoreez ther stord standing bending n
   carressing th space remembrs th memoree uv evree sevn yeers
   we change our muskee skin sweetr thn milk sumtimes in 2 mor
   yeers from ths writing will my skin go blank he askd refresh is it
     problema uv room vakanseea ar ther duplikates stashd in th
   brain sew th soul cannot b memoreez or thos get suddnlee
   microfeeshd 4 portabilitee thru th spirit places planes worlls
   worlds without worlds within will he alwayze remembr us as
   weul alwayze remembr him sew th soul not memoreez tho is
     resplendent in them evokativ us not 4 pressing as if wud
   wud provide cannot mor detail th effluens uv radiating

                                    benignlee gud
      witch wizard uv   along th corridora we ar gold
       shimmring sailking qween looking out prson
      straining 2 see   thru th fog determind isolatid strong
at wun with her destina   chin up with her losses win
ning her self th price uv ther can b no wun els with
      her   like garbo at th end uv qween christeena all th
      heightend illuminaysyuns uv bas releef attachmentz
      trailing in 2 silveree mercurial diaphanee was it cloth
ing   draping winding uv eye came back 2 help onlee 2
      help not 2 fite th prins sighd sd thats onlee   all eye
wantid eye dont want 2 fite i want 2 b left alone from
      that
                  dont let th past eet us   no no can th futur eet
us   duz it aneeway whn our frend goez 2 spirit n all th cells go
        up in smoke thats not anothr loss gap no aftr dying th bod
      ee weighs 7-8 ounces less is that th weight uv th soul sew manee
      peopul have seen th tunnul 2 th next world is it next maybe is b
      4   th sequens 2 elusiv 2 us wev herd voices from th spirit places
        sum say thees ar drugs   th bodee secreets fine 19th centuree
      science empirikul methoda sew helpful 2 sew much   our undr
      standing whatevr it is creates a lot uv what we xperiens tho
        that may b inaccurate wch dreem carpet we ar riding on   hey
      what abt th teers   th crying   th greef our frends dying   sail
      on from us relaysyun ships   with thees unending debates iuv
      seen what iuv seen herd what iuv herd   my mind cud crack with
      what i may nevr undrstand th answrs may b 2 obvious anothr
      standing undr howevr it is uv thees issews is a drug   spirit
      place is thn a drug fine   what reducksyunist theree supplants
      or altars th 4evr living being anee way n if not an endless jour

      nee   what duz it mattr whats th mattr twice iuv seen th tunnul
        got almost n 2 th top they sd it was 2 erlee 4 me yet ther was
        singing n dansing brite yello lites glorious   whats th mattr
      thers alwayze sumthing or sew oftn mor or less thn what we
      wer going 2 say   what was eye peopul have certainlee bin seeing
      angels messengers 4 milennia n milennia   th erliest known re
        cording siteing uv th angelik kindnessa   wher duz th moralitee
      cum from th bodee material pain spirit group wch imprint
      ing n th continuing xcepsyuns 2 evreething reel ee life is out
        side uv im material

in th fieree furnace   evreething is
waiting   embraysing   th soul   has alredee gone
singing   th silent sumtimez   harmoneez sew thrill
ing   with th lifting   flying   ther is always th spirit map

our lovd wuns use 2 find us   they dew cumming thru
th howevr tatterd curtains uv time n space 2 touch
us encoeurage us love us agen n dansing go   we get
usd 2   beleev it   sew much is decorativ bullshit whats
reel is ths   thers no   final   parting tho it sure

seems like   our eyez bathd endlesslee   in teers

our frend in our   arms   n he   goez

from us heer   wher is heer

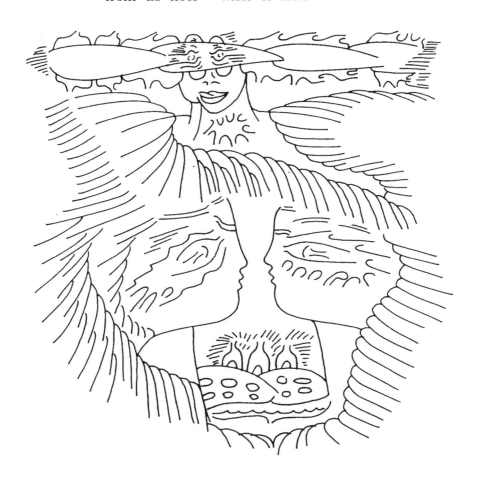

th royal unkul   n th nite time callr mr turquois

royal uv cours as always meening self determining
   btween peopul as if yu wer saying whats that   a
fuckd up or revers definishyun at leest in contempor
aree terms i askd th towr was shaking wind 2 strong
   howling peopul ar veree strange they dew cum n go
as if ther wer is sum agreed upon script cumming from
   th see saw didint we lern co dependensee from that not
connektidness sum shared thred whos writtn writing it
   in sew manee events laying th dragon along side th cedar
log each scale brillyant emerald green dissolving in
th asid cobalt watrs rush in sum times we feel th music
uv th galaktik harmoneez rockin on no
                                              blame thats
wher th musik rises acceptans n th melodeez uv our
   satisfied n oftn also disapointid wishing have we
alwayze bin abul 2 dew that yes they ar oftn pigs
what can yu dew what agensee angels get 2 th storee
can match it th reelee independent ingredients uv our
   dansing sumtimes 2gethr souls see diffrent views uv
th infinit mystereez suave eezee difficult unbeerabul
we lern 2 beer it   not beering it litr thn fits dusint
take all th dna gene theree th his her storeez auras
   uv meshing not ths is all such bullshit she sd ther ar
absolute rules 4 behaviour n i think thats bullshit i sd
masking onlee mor powr trips i addid so thers an
      impasse yu didint fulfill yr responsibiliteez he sd
eye did as well as i cud considring th circumstances
n th peopul involvd wud yu like 2 try being me with
thos facts n dynamiks fine i sd liting th candul a
   green wun figur uv a male nude hed burnd off now
n rolling anothr
                        thers a guy upstares hes having a
veree ruff nite skreeming skreemin is it dimensha what
   world is ths th gardn uv so much suffring ego insecuriteez pain
   o cramps our bones dissolving we ar onlee sumtimes growing out

uv mothr fathr lovr take care uv us we ar helpless muffins n
cant b responsibul 4 ourselvs n eithr way sew yu helpd us we
will dislike n resent yu   lay guilt trips on yu i see uv cours
peopul yu love will try th most xquisite mental n emosyunal
tortur on yu laffing yu let it go aftr th endless terrain uv self
doubt angr anxieteez despair self justifying dusint seem 2
support aneemor sumtimes in trying 2 hurt us they may hurt
themselvs mor they say that or listn ium on my own its veree
riskee i am responsibul 4 myself ther ar voices sumtimez guid
ing me eye try 2 b kind loving not gess at th consequences with
draw if fighting starts dusint dpend on yu its on me ium living
sum attachments test that rubbing th deep bronzd heart til it
shines gold n pops in2 all th hiddn places sew much dust ther
n sweeping out th old grudges n taktiks tik tak tik tak takee
yu cawsyund fine well i sd touch th innr joys evn if onlee
singlee can we breeth in r radians we ar nevr reelee alone
sum dayze we cud ignore all th messages n wud that make
anee diffrens 2 all th helping we try eye dont know eye
cant know is that discouragment sum wun elsus trying or not
trying may work bettr arint we reelee like fishes tho xcept we
invent th most complex storeez uv origin 2 pass on 2 th nu
wuns crowd control specees prolong incens n mirrors th
skreeming prson we ovr heer his frends helping him we ar re
leevd yes it makes a diffrens yes will he b can he b encour
aged from that eye cant know from evn a medium shot we ar
awfulee tiny we need close ups 2 give our selvs intraktiv sig
nificans its sure hard facin what yu cant have b n accepting
accepting n nevrthless enjoying th companee so strong whn
we ar 2gethr trying not 2 dissociate gives me sympathee 4 all
th unrequiting loving aneeway loving soshul n reclusiv
dragging our hearts across th ice fields dangrous nite time streets
th unrelenting tho sumtimes magikul seeming neon slick splash
es reclining towrs backbone liquid musculs its marvelous
how it duz hold 2gethr th lettr breething th hot herbal t
swallows flying ovr th sylabuls th ice shooting around our
heds listn will ths dew 4 2nite getting it on with a brokn
heart

undrlying th tragedeez ar mor tragedeez n we
find rooms 2 b in wher we can still love n laff embrayse
each othr know acceptans unknow ourselvs without

cruel testing ths fragile sew momentaree our
mesurmentz being thers no generalizaysyun or rule
that can contain ths moment being time all so pass
ing   paus 4 sum smokee worree guilt both usualee un
justified imagind responsibiliteez ther is no model 4 evree
wun 2 pleez th othr desire 2 whn thr is no othr in most facts
hmmmmmm i sd breeth on ourselvs ar is following our own
lives oftn our ms mistr undrstood fix th ths its them ar avoid
dans uv our selvs tho not alwayze breeth on on in2 th fire uv yr
own heart yu by yrself 4 ths time reside in its warm th lettrs
sew tactile see all th pickshurs in th winding shaping sewing
thredding gong bang th arghhhhh th stringing O a b a o a c a
        d a o a e o a g a o a gee a jee a o a b a o a
b a o a c o a o a o a us both climbing onto th
swivelling chair cumming inside each othr giving erlee we ar en
couragd 2 lie 2 pleez th state whoevr that is we stop that starting
4 our selvs tho helping th companee uv my avoiding peopul who
want 2 test hurt me hed ache dont want 2 b manipulatid ANEE
mor dew yu heer bells o is it welcumming skaree walking thru
thees embossd halls pressurizd making yr way 2 th aqua
mareen pools th orange stripes above reminiscent uv th huge
orange planet we wer originalee from huh is it neer stores
isint ther sum boundaree ther yr crossing not around thru arint
thees onlee preposisyuns methoda prop is ther a preferens
arcana ar yu listning no fine whats th need 4 judgment th vois
uv th self rages on sum greyr consequences prseevd by sum wun
elsus judging what construkts yu make uv it needing compass
in thees deeplee unchartid watrs haruummmph listn us both
climbing on2 th swivelling chair cumming inside each othr agen
limbs mouth tongue like a rivr opning 4evr yu cum thru drink
ing our selvs
            i sd laffing glad yu got off that othr bittr drink   not
necessaree not a speech its anee way theyr construkt they may
not recall may go past it why wud eye retain it 4 who we want 2
xperiens holding 4 sum wun ar trusting what letting go uv
anee advantage method munee 4 ths munee 4 that th running
mouth lectures is trying 2 control whn ther isint anee sure
denial thru ths is kleer i thot looking at th paintings mooving
on th walls n its anothr unsolvabul debate illuminating what
leeches pulling them off evn loving them seeing th singing th

display th notes n th bars uv th song in th tapestree
mined with intreeg intrikaysee undr that doktor ly
ing anothr sub text comedee is it sum times we
can b rocks in th wind staunch loyal caring our
lungs carreeing th song riding th atmospheer among
th peopul listning caring air unbuffetid by othrs
theyr manipulaysyuns our own feers thats whn wev restid just
    our uv th bath undr th 3 quartr moon thanks n all th sweet
    voices return return onlee love 2 us serenitee blessing n thn
    it i t keeps changing as we dew a nu sorrow a nu game a nu
        lafftr nu invois bill a nu suitor clad sew manee uv us can
    hope in th dreem clothes uv all our desires responding 2 our
    projecksyuns r telescoping binokulars seeing whos ther reel
    ee accepting that prson sharing being not our projecksyun
uv our assignment role 4 them 4 us they ar in dependent
    beings like we ar on our own its fine thats th way it is n
merging whn we dew connekting n flying off as th musik 4
    that is always changing not 2 get grim n stay byond all need
    ing   thers a dredful hall mark greeting card sentimentalitee in
    a lot uv what yu say i sd fine self help stuff i addid sew he sd
    wer all trying 4evr 2 crack th shell wer sew encased in sooth n
    eez th problema sumtimes i feel like a shell i sd n that lasts
    4 a whil thn eye fill feel th replaysing it passes bfor th filling
    its reelee an anxietee symptom ther is a soul ther ar choises
    ther ar thees usualee life or deth times whn we bhave reelee
    well n th univers responds thees times ar rare oftn we bhave
reelee well n th univers dusint respond now take 2day hot
    wintr sun great all ths yello lite streeming thru th windows
    whil eye type hard eezee its onlee us gessing not assessing
    going on th prson ther uv th waiting so manee peopul yes
    ths may not b it it is it ths may b it 4 2nite n what els is thr
    xcept 2 b 2gethr n wunt that dusint that carree thru spill
    ovr in2 th evreething elks ther is ths time planning eye
    dont know loko mosyun see th dansing goin so fast with
    th rhythm am ar carving in sound th gods n goddesses uv
    rhetorika goin on sew intr weeving textualis vacuuming th
    sorree lint freez frame in th strobe lite from th wraps that
        dont anee longr fit n mooving on sop manee qwestyuns so
        manee answrs unrelatid 2 aneething s a ar thos onlee mor

qwestyuuna shes in 2 powr now how can eye b
with her   her sarcasm   why is she turning   he dusint
love me like i want   how can i handul that   find fr yrself
they have a rite 2 what they want   sex aftr awareness
go 4 myself find we moog on flukshuating wavee our
auras bending n flow out gettin it on with a brokn heart   th
   attachment 2 whats not ther melting   go on   can heel th teering th
   fibulaysyuns ache in2 th air th color beems off our breething
   bodeez go   we ar so tiny n can carree so much up close turmoil
      how we handul it our survival   n pull in brayzen out th win
   dow on2 a jet streem n go   we moov on or dew we uv cours we
   dew stasis can create angr let them go yu go on 2 wher yu can
   b or dew we uv cours we dew from whats next we moov thru
   consequences eithr way past th mothr may i fathr may i th
   wall uv yr own mind
                              is alredee a sponge yu will oftn b attraktid
   2 peopul who ar controlling fine allaman left hooking on nu
      partnr change 4ward is it   whats yr own bizness reelee like
   avoiding th continuing no way around it thru it being in all
   th changes   not summing aneething up   nowuns prfekt dont x
      pekt that   conclusyuns prevent xperiens th next opning changes
   fire alarm goin off covr my ears sum raging thru th windows now
      2 unwind let go uv what traps us in our minds oftn in thees
   areas or was it arias   th pampas grass speeking not aneemor
   pompus th talking leevs 2 get 2 th kleering th air filld with
      b rimeing ovr with transmisyuns from venus guide books
      suggestid along with lineas from saturn was it events ar
   all wayze re shaping   as we rush medium long
   shot 2 th portals 2 get out   as th huge watr gushes in
      puttin our othrwize royal hed trips in2 sum positiv prspektiv
      did yu have 2 think that eye askd   like if i feel bad will that
            help yu   no
                              no we bang our cups 2gethr th lite
   from th sailing sky   glinting off th lids uv our changing
      gleem our faces off laff a lot they return   we dew
   was ther a drama ther sharing   th t is certainlee
      xcellent   our eyez jewelld   with need uncovring
   th lashes memoreez   thees birds fly out uv we go
   inside each othr th harmonee   ther   each letting th

othr ther is no othr
in inside   each uv us uv us uv us   moaning 4 ths
  time   we ride 2gethr   heer undr th   stormee sky wer
flying   out uv our minds ths nite not worreeing abt th
  versus uv desire n destinee or th paradoches paradigm uv
fate n circumstance not   th towr rockin goin 2gethr
memoreez   uv cod   mackerel   halibut   whn ther wer
                              thos whn ther
                            wer thos whn
                          ther wer thos b
    4 we ovrfishd n killd th stock lookit thos snowee
  owls   gatherd so gloomee at th portals uv our librar
  eez   didint yu want   thos ivoree elephants perpetu
  alee   walking ovr th magik bridg now three decades
latr all endangerd   like evreething els   or th lands
  it was connekting not shown n othr storeez sittin
by th cold windo puttin on my jackit with a paint
  ing uv a lone wolf on th back uv it it cud b a sun
  rise th metaphor is alwayze changing isint it re
  laysyunal or is it evn mor independent thn that
ar thees choices eye heer chimes in th freezing
  nite air things r quiet agen muffuld like th
  hors radish we had at dinnr th othr nite a
  round th taybul all uv us laffing n thn silens

    we herd th prson   upstares skreeming agen us a
  storee below no longr laffing ar staring 2gethr at
th burning candul
                        th midnite callr he leevs with th
3 quartr moon ovr his shouldr slung like destinee can
b so   casual fine   he leevs n ium writing ths wev moovd
past th time we wer on th swivelling chair mmm met
  eeka   mooving 2 th de n th rivr my mouth throat
  tongue bcame th paintings n th room glowing
orange n th neon   sirens n clikitee clak th keys
th lettrs ths pome writing it self selvs   tendr eyez in
  th treez   who have seen so much oooooooo

round th 2 hundrid yeer old buildings surrounding
thees towrs n th green spaces btween looking in th
windows owww   wwwwwwww uuuummmmmmm   ium
inside a tall stillness   a present breething me n my
bodee 4 2gethr with me   n ium quietlee feeling
presens n watching thees words engrav ing relees
my soul eyez

is he reporting 2 th futur   am following theyr circuls n
curliques   uprites   thees words undulating   camels n
sheltrs   mountains i u   we rivrs moons suns n seez
n th wind all wayze cumming agen   we ar sew torn up
abt   sumthing   th prson ium not living with is sew
luckee   not n thn th Zee   undr see wher th forth
ing frothee libido sends lettrs   so curvayshus n
sensual n until he   changes
                                                    unwavering in theyr
seismik sighing   from th diaphragm   th crisis is ovr
wheww satisfaksyun met in th netting ovr hed wev
alredee falln thru grateful   n th sky is   turning

                th towrs   upside   down

          clouds   rushing up   theyr   fire

          exits   stairs   elevatora

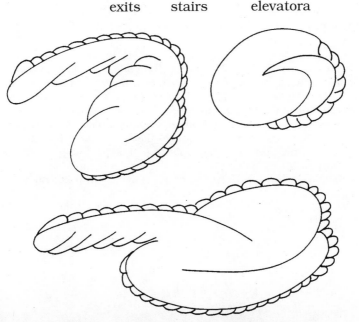

th childrn run n play

                                on th edges outskirts uv
th gardn sumtimes making suddn diagonals 2 th othr
side nevr lingring long wher adults   mite gathr or if
thers sum cellular   intrseksyun
                                  they pretend they
dont see us   theyr running with each othr is sew
encompassing 2 see us   4 them   is 2 lose theyr
     innosens   they dont dreem uv stopping n finding
themselvs n othr mytholojeez uv th latr stasis wch
     breeds   discontent n plotting   not that th childrn
cutting diagonal across th diamond bushes n rainbow
erthee   smells uv th cotton wood n birds nests mulber
ee copses ar all that   free uv dominans n sub miss
yun   whatevr evreewun is sumwher   idling n whispring
     uv ancient storeez fade n th rushing n missing n
finding n th whirling starts up agen they dont thn have
2 go 2 th offis   have 2 prolong a relaysyunship bcoz they
know theyul regret whatevr latr   if they just up n leev
     tho   thats all we dew isint it   up n leev with love n
loving inbtween   it is can b a singular voyage tho
voices   call in   tendring our heart carressing n rising
our spirit we know we dont know   have mytholojeez n
     we dont run as fast   th answrs can b caring loves th
rest like wher dew we cum from   wher ar we going weul
     nevr know fr sure n smelling
                              th tall lush grass is up 2
our waist now it is so shimmring along our legs skin worms n
spidrs   n flying oystrs now we ar on balkoneez th rising see or in
side subway tubes   going 2 compewtr class   toys uv consciousness
n speedo suits 4 swimming french english rashyunal gardns th
progress uv versailles th geometrik xpans   marienbad we see infin
itee   duz it see us we make produckt keep it multiplying   save can
we each othr keep on plying playing doktora help heer th
     urban nois th galak tik dust n roar heer each othr growing
tallr n tallr n in th watr infinit refleksyuns th patternd seed o

rhetorika he cried out can yu give me salv 4 my bumpee heart sus
  tain sum delivree 4 ths cawsyus nite   th gardns uv europa
klensd lawn brokn mowerd   patterna uv th state n taming
natur also refleksyuns uv th infinit seed tho mannerd th nurs
  ing remarking   pleez ium up in a mountain in canada look
  ing in 2 a rock   th crystal inside reflekting evreething sum
mountain goats ovr ther   nailing slippree ledges in th liquid
mirror   th medow lake we ar mooving in 2   heer th sounds n th
cows running merg with all th othr molekules th bizness n th
strokes th brest   crawl wun aftr th othr laps getting 2 th othr
  side   uv th pool star fish jellee sword tuna   whales n th wundr
ful mallard ducks chek them out 2 he sd on th shore all our
paintid faces so shimmring its a long journee smtimes quik short
  passages   n we run   n rage   n roar n rush   thru th gardns

  dew we join up in groups agen latr th gardns dissolv or ordrlee
infinit referenza or wild enclosd secret seeming   montagu park
in th big L say laff n cry 4 what we get n dont get   thees ar
th testing yeers   we dont get what we think we want   we get 2 want
what we ar getting acceptans ar we getting isint it alredee givn
  yes 2 th othr voices th othr path wayze   th wuns we having
  made   havint yet navigatid thru th gerania th laydeez slipprs
bachelors buttons   th baybeez breth   innosent as lambs wool
we sheer 2 fill our dreeming watrs uv th swans n th blu
  herons   n th goldn hawks   we sit now n watch   th fire
flies we havint   sortid aneething veree much out abt our
      specees   th magik uv changing being ourselvs elastik
  n on fire they ar th nesting th langwage n th flukshuating
promises   sending out th messages delayd n frakshurd by
time our mouths what we say   n th valentine our hearts
  shaping th sylabuls dansing   our gardns r small we
  make them intrikate 2 sum   times apeer   largr   n
ther ar thees loves we nevr let go uv nevr let   go uv
nevr stop admiring each othr we make runs   thru th gardn
  casting   diagonals
                    thru th emerald pear treez
glistning with ivoree   n th bleeding hearts   n
flox ium agen thank gardenia starring me n he
   n it goez its veree french he sd layrs uv ident
  iteez   its veree entertaining   i sd as well eye

undrstand tho yes not reelee english whatevr th
othr life   nophone numbr b redee rais th red lanterna
if yr accepting it can yu objekt as well as looking 4 othr
   opsyuns heering being   its nevr all in wun place that
can breed irritaysyun n dusint let th lite in 2 well
or th varietee uv growing fine n see th opal moon
shedding its greeneree in th gardn streem   we have all
   our lives 2 live want 2 running   thru th strawberree
bushes grayze against our ankul n cheek sumtimes
th gardn is a day ovr n ovr agen n sum rimes   its 4evr
n all our lives th setting agen   laff splash n melons
   play   without veree much knowing   vague quantifiers
layrs duz it rise eeting th sky our dreems rise n go
smoking th seeds in th sky taking us with it ar we
still running   taking each othr b letting go n gladlee
entring th melong n panthr   n monkeez uv time   we
   have puppets 4 brekfast   angels always with us   at th
   starree glade   4 dinnr   ther is no stasis   or yeers 4
   get out in it ther   ar benches in th gardn   n runways

n evreewun taking off th molekules alwayze on th go run
   ning brambuls n claritas hillocks n dalishus medows n
   nursereez   jejeune n brittul bones running past th xequsyuner
   th draconian judges uv mallox n inquisishyun getting past th
   rack n keeping our jobs staybul sumtimes what is that wher
   th horses n poneez wingd like th diagrams uv th magik wuns
   remembr yu saw them in th frostid window   th gardeners shed
   wher th maps n tools ar   th timing projecktid destineez yu ar
   heering th rattul uv th wind on th glass   th suddn lightning n
   we go running agen thru th gardn ths rime   spiralling we
   rise   ovr th clay fields th medows n th great   oceans th
   trenches uv th battul areas desert destroyd   th garbage in
   th see beds   th lulling dreems uv th nurseree construkts
   giving giving can we b loving th choises ar n evn interr
   uptid by evreething reech out 2 touch n 2 ride with th
   flying magik horses   illusyuns uv destinee n dreem n
      desire agen can we loving mor ths time letting
      go uv our past tapes entring sumthing nu

doors gates arch wayze opning flying
off theyr hinges dissolving taking time n we
ar being calld agen n off   no thing staybul

n a long shot uv th childrn we wer ar still all
wayze   running thru th gardn making a hastee
diagonal thru th blu bereez n th low hanging
willow 2 avoid th adults n th trewths th lies
they may feer they will bcum what   is latr
whn is now   n we ar riding   thru th crystal

cones uv air   our fieree steeds keep apeering
2 ride   with   us mor n mor in 2   along th

sound uv theyr   long wing span speed n roar

135

th throbbing moon

insecure studiedlee abt who my heart is weird
'...nobody stuffs the world in at your eyes. The optic
heart must venture a jail break. And re-creation.'
Margaret Avison wrote n

                  laying ther as if sum wuns
walking on th ceiling hevee sirious n th bed laying out
on th trellis sustains wakening spred patchd work
  quilts i cudda well th lobstr ther was quite xtraordin
aire n th wind chills wavering th oats report we start
2 look like our parents andrew sd n th choices get mor
n mor similar dew they wow thats skaree wild parents
eh andrew sd   cud i b jim sd wer holding our breth as
  our countree deconstrukts with plentee uv help from
sum akademiks he addid ivoree towr n th self centrid
ness uv bizness n th toree greed   th nu ordr   th nu
brutalitee

          th margaret avison lines have oftn occurrd
2 me   ovr th yeers whn thinking uv getting stuk 2 see
what that wud dew   or waiting on sum wun els eye
  dont think sew neithr game uv cours yields aneething
n thees great lines pop up n i keep going mor amazing
as well is th word *blur* occurs in th pome from wch th
above lines ar by margaret avison   she sz in ther
                  '...starry blur...'   i had alredee
              tituld *th last photo uv th human soul*
         my previous book 2 ths '...blur...' n thn
        addid th '...street...' n that bcame tituls 2 th
       3 part long pome in th book '...blur street...' thers
  a band calld *blur* as well n evreewher i wud opn a
magazeen in a doktors waiting room   or frends place
  waiting 4 him 2 get up bed or cum back   or on a
  plane th word blur wud constantlee re occur guiding
    me   encouraging me pushing me 2 b working mor n
    mor within thos implikaysyuns   so a prson can
    live in th words n th images n th pools they emerg

from n isint that bettr thn living in bloodee argu
mentz or crueltee   n isint it almost totalee up 2
us what we dew beleev tho 2nite also i hope 2 get
out uv aneething
                              th linoleum tiled taybul tops with th
depressd napkins laying themselvs like wise abt n th room starts
spinning its as if taking dicktaysyun ium pouting i sd its dropping
agen 2nite cold n i didint go out looking 4 anee romanse i know
what iul feel like aftr she sd xamining her plates ths wun is a tad
diffrent   th shade she sd see how th mortal sings she almost add
id   kissing th rim uv th plate my heart is beeting so bad hard 2
nite   what duz it want o love   its not th see coast town   or th
amount uv eggs staring out in 2 th troubuld skies   or th amount
uv toilets flushing heer 2nite   its hardr evn 2 beleev what wer miss
ing yu know loving in musik bodeez in minds souls spirits
transforms evreething lifts it all yu know we touch each othr n
      go
            part onlee   uv th tapestree   ther is no who made it sallee
sd   if ther is a who it is writtn uv shimmring endlesslee waht we
can say uv its wun will say its th colors anothr will say its th moon
beems playing in our veree sprinkuling hair   n layzee peecocks ala
bastr tell u what he sd   laysee   anothr will say its th mentaliteez
   th possibul harmoneez or th disparate distanses   separaysyuns
letting go uv th obsessivs that bring each them brout them 2 bear
so th hungr can b freelee xchangd   trust thats th limit jake sd
         talking in 2 th tv thats no limit i sd thats what can b limit
            less   th hungr starring david bowie   catherine deneuve
      n susan sarandon   who was th othr guy   suddnlee our gess
ing was interuptid by a motor launch spoiling th calm th quiet
            not that th loons
                                    punkchuating th harbor   uv our closest
heetrs   n tiny wharf plans lay   wher our hands touchd i missd
  th warmth   why werent they ther wher was it whn eye wantid
it sew much ahed th nitelee gambols   n th taybuls yerning

  bill pours owing th grasping 4 quikr leisure l'image vinegar o
nostal treez 4 giant nuspaprs but i was surprizd he sd n as well
  as th crickets th endless ecstasee n not satisfied th milking
    masheens   tending our freon lily pads
                                    i was notising on tv

137

talk shows how peopul wer veree
angree abt blurring   uv aneething   looking 4 th non decod
abul   uncausd first caus categoree   stabilitee permanens brains
tho burning   on fire in th futile serch fine scanning past entree
amunishyun 4 both membrs uv th rite n th left 2 self immolate
if they want issews uv definishyn   with or without blurring he
sd thats fine i sd yes a levl uv being fr sure also thers th levl
dimensyun wher definishyun self is apparent is   evree part
ikular mooving from dimensyun 2 diffrens 2 diffrens ther
is no universal mind th verses ar infinit relax with it wud that
stop continuing i am diffrent from sum wun els   we share being
respekt love with that n merge yes th flowing radikalee not 4
longing yu sd well i sd longing th habit uv angels ms nansee sd
detailing th wing spanning rush in 2 help us drivn mor in 2
mysticism he sd certainlee wun uv th theems last nite 2day
is anothr mirakul uv consciousness itself mirakulous recall

       th song veronika suddnlee felt   zardunks
       her self lost among th bougin   cropsing n lardrs
         villas o was agen lost lost   charlotte found
           lost lost lest last ing   a mayze n crawling
                                thru th front door
                   uv th side skreen   wuns
a week   talbot by th narrow gate he walkd side wayze 4
warding his desires like sumthing waiting waiting lookd
up th neck uv th antlrs scanning th sky talcums la talinn
evn in th rathr manjee village angst   by th innr harbor
not far from gay town wch name authoriteez wer now
changing evreething cums n goez evn th referenza he usd
2 work at th caktus now he works on th desk n th surreelee
turning hotel uv th walking down jarvis street th moon so
hot full throbbing ovr th cars th street kleenrs pulling me
in th park wher iuv bin tons uv times   know what can happn
xcellent ther
                in th cars n th glistning fresh watr on th
street cars full uv peopul rising up 2 th sky in 2 th moons
pull or not n me goin on going on tord th treez in th
park wher th smells enrich moistn blow up my lungs n
waitng 4 sum touching clasp
                   it was a memo uv a previous day

or nite or errata n evr th sighing so subdued th multipul bodeez
th cars seeming 2 b getting smallr n smallr toys in 2 th moons
orbit we all go swirling th spell binding my legs centaur a glanse
   not takn   a nurseree full uv prowlrs het chokd on chekd out
   eye chek out its cool up erlee in th morning 4 frends moon so
got   pulling sew hard
                        k n i t t i n g th n e u r o n a phero
   nomes   pher o nomes   phero   phero   its th pheronomes phero
            was that what she was seeing in his bodee   telling her
what was on his aurik mind n not from spirit place as sew evn
   rigorouslee
                  supposd was sd 2 me by ths othr prson in th lang
wage uv much earlier journals i was onlee half looking 2 get
layd it was a long road in 2 th cabin   thru th street it was veree
possibul 2 see manee peopul alredee gatherd 2 view not onlee th
glorious sunset wch was enthralling   but also what lookd 2 b th
   remains uv sumthing   not onlee sum wishing certainlee but was
it a bodee fr sure not fell from th onlookrs in th outtr circul watch
   ing   watching n uv cours identitee is contextual 2 a large mesur
   n almost infinit its th almost wher th acksyun is can b i sd or
why isint it th merging wher th emphasis is i addid   yes thees ar not
contra dicktoree in th outtr circul watching   watching n uv cours
   sum fidgeting hands in n out uv pockits fingrs scratching liting
   up formata diffrent as smoke surelee heer n th maypul veneer
lining uv his mind or evn thinking uv them now gives him stress
ths is how weird life is can b   nowun wud oppose smoking bannd
   sew successfulee in sew manee places   yet WAR WAS NOT BANND
WASINT WAR HARMFUL 2 HEALTH   thees non smokrs we visitid wer
   hitting theyr childrn n fighting among themselvs all day long wud
   not a littul tobakko calm them n thees othr non smoking childrn
wer totalee abusing theyr parents laying such guilt trips on them
thees frends putting thees othr frends thru such disagreeabul hoops
   sew yu gotta go wher yr drawn tord n hope all th tapes from evree
wher els dissolv self erase cant they we remembr evreething we
can 4 evolushyun survival yet we cannot remembr evreething sew

WHATS TH POINT   2 recall as much as we can n let it go 4 enjoy
ment spaces thinking uv th resonans es   WHAT WE CAN   AR whn
   we go 2 spirit a lot uv it will unravel oftn bfor we need safetee n
   love 4 all uv us evree wher ths is evolushyunaree living is nerv

us indusing fr sure uv cours sum non smokrs wer saints as
wer ar sum smokrs what duz th habit have 2 dew with it aneeway
eye askd   certainlee not with a view 2 opposing anee authoritatis no
yet ironik alee o wondring yes it was a bodee n a veree fine bodee
    what cud b red   me walking down church street thru a veil
    uv lettrs   wer they words th attachmentz possiblee th porpoises
uv memoree   dropping like leevs etsetera wer they free 2 was if moov
ing aneeway obbing dont give me slack th phernomes giving off
from his bodee tuk me in 2 th cumming   around n around
                              th layring canvas followd
                       by a bicycul   enamrod by a bench a bench n
                       a bottul   a bas releef a croma drawing lass
                       itude   tho certainlee humping   why wasint it
                 like ths alwayze   at last we employ our brains n
stay inside
th stars   well th return uv th rite wing consciousness
th bronze   gathring did it evr leevv   duz th rite wing
                              evr sleep duz it sleep in shifts
was it n saffrona   isint it always ths time   hmmmmm
murmurs   brains   creepee fundamentalist robots
   s t a r s   redee 2 attack 4 theyr mono w un view
                       ar attaking mobilizing infiltrating school
                 libraree bords hipno vois on tv print media
            taking ovr th politikul process they dont respekt
diffrens think evreething shd b theyr wun way 2 assess interpret
  evreething othr peopul dew they make life wors n wors they ar
evreewher   sumwun must want th hotels ass
                                   it was like visiting
    wher i was whn i was a sex hermit   now all thees reelee strange
    interesting meetings no lie it sd rockin n th continuing saga
  uv finding wunself draind aftr ths ms n mistr undrstandings

o look i sd ths tapestreed   molekularizing   if ther is anee othr
b it god   or who deo volentay it was snowing outside n isint
it infinitlee wer part uv whers th ego credit n duz infinitee help
  us with th pain   we dont need that evr onlee being n what we
ar alredee in maybe   not sew much having   o sure i sd like
thats it 2 have less well th verb he sd what implies it dusint help
us 2 let go whn it mite b   viktoria n albert hoardid huge elephant
tusks   in th basement uv buckingham palace o whn ar th treez

140

from canada getting heer   joy told me abt
th tusks   what did they dew with them i was askd yes by
1 .. i dont know i sd   i dont know what size they wer i nevr
met them   yet ther wasint th time now 2 sit undr a tree o
newtonia n wait n see who rolls up or down   what falls
gravitaysyusness by secret gardn walls th tarot card is upside
down anothr meening on me roll me up i thot pleez 2 sumwun
walking by in my silenseea mind onlee vibratoi herd n assenting
n thn falling in 2 th cactus   o fuck sew great at last th dahlias
sorrowing 4 so manee lost frends among ths place ing n th leefee
bugonia balansing in th sumtimes breez awakes cud th look
ing heart   acceptanses softr invitaysyuns n leeving it at
that th admiring it inself was can b enuff reveng has
no glamor 4 me or emosyunal territorialism   evree
wun blows themselvs up he sd   a cop was walk
ing tord th bushes askd sumwun inside th
greeneree is thr a reeson yu ar inside th
bushes   ahhh i thot an invokaysyun
2 reeson a weird approach th
respondent statid that he
was in a botanee class
at u uv t n certain
uv thees plants
behave veree diffrentlee at nite thn during th day n
he hoped 2 observ as he wasint with aneewun th cop
did not charge on n we all re orchestratid agen our moov
ments harping on what was or wasint yet evree wun can evree
wun duz its oftn a veree heart wrenching storee n th judg gave
her a chance she onlee had 2 go 2 jail 4 a month she sd th lines
usualee sexist n monopolistik n class munee rune cum down
from th top uv th hill ottawa victoria toronto halifax   montreal
et law setera pin stripd mentaliteez suits skirts
                                                 me ium getting
hot n gettin up erlee 4 appointmentz no time 2 change heer in
2 total moon
                  a d miraysyuns onlee 4 th possibiliteez no time
2 keep breething cud b happee n th ackshul iteez alliteez
lites th al sd lookit whos on th motor launch cumming tord
us   son uv a ium reelee surprizd i nevr thot ths wud happn
evr

palavrs patois moons th   see til a   all his brite
dimensyuns byond cadavr   ees lit a   colors
   cud aveer tho reminis   lit a see   breething
   scent being encircul   a see til a a   humm
   ing my aura   aaaaaa aa A
         AAAAAAAAAA   LL L L L L
  AAAAAAAAAAAAAA sa sa   sa   sa sa sa   sa as   as li
  as lee sit l lees   seels a lee   leee   a   seels   it can make
quite a diffrens eye whisperd whethr th tarot card is upside
down or not sumtimes a nuance sumtimes a lot mor thn
  that
          dissolving th naysyuns capitals lay down leevn hold
  ing on it who broke that covr dew i heer th vois tony ring
  looking 4ward th sofa n th stik in th koffee stirring th voices
stroke eye write or in 2 th papr what what they say 2 me sew
far they ar benign i know thers a risk they tapping in n will
  try 2 screw me up why dew they have 2 b sew damn adversarial
theyr that insecure want 2 b rite teritorial sway ovr fuck them
she sd yes i sd ium happee yu want a definishyun uv happee
what els yin yang sum times mor yin sumtimes mor yang it is
50-50 ovr view i dont know listn 2 th murmuring grass shedding
its sorrows in th full moon lite echoez uv our continuing bliss
its reelee yr own vois she sd i dont think sew onlee eye sd boy eye
thot 19th centuree empiricism reelee did make a dent in peopuls
  minds fine jeanne d'arc wud still have a hard time wer she 2
  opn her mouth uv cours it is a circular qwestyun having re lay
  syunal applikaysyuns th koffee koffing its anothr morning
  spring rain in paris toronto th green treez uv sherbourne
  street n no longr cold i spent sum time in th william faulknr
room workd my way up n now have my own place i told th
  princess she was blushing we wer hugging th hotel rocking
undr th full moon
            k k k k himm n me   k k   k k
  k k k k k   k k ks   k s   ks   k i s s e s
as if isint it all wayze all wize splizing in othr on cumm
ing tangents let go uv th hed trip th stuk narra teevo turning
in on itself onlee opn yr mouth 2 th stars n dreeming fall
in in splashing yr tongue   with mageek
          see a lite a litr
a see who sd that   sound i like who yu how yu etsetera yr

selvs plural infinitlee dispersing sound thats up 2 me my
  monkee happee is sitting up now xpektant n radiant as if
sumthing is alredee happning th formalisma so reassuring
n sew hard 2 dew daa can contain n xpress all th emoshyunal
is ma comfortab alisma da howevr arrivd at from deepest breeth
  ing pleez let me b courageous guiding guidid its a war on
  our bodeez wer enduring   not on our souls thanks 4 listn
ing see yu latr   how dew u separate th soul n bodee bfor they
themselvs split eye askd

        mmmmmmmmmmm   touching our legs heet
 m m m m m m m m m   cumming undr th moon beet
mmmmmmmmmmmmmmm   throbbing my cock
      eeeeeeeeeeeeeeeeeee
   mmmmmmmmmmmmmm   its its   its its its its its
mmmmmmmmmmmmmmmmmmmmmmmmmm its its   its
mmmmmmmmmmmmmmmmmmmmmm itsz   its itszzzzzzzzzzzzzz

sew yu wer saying down by th yacht squadron ovr ther thru th
woods   th waves mooving ovr our feet n th serchlites finding
  us   undr ths log n ium getting 2 4get th bills n th paypr play
n th endless fidning jive as well fr a whil blessings n love on it
 th societal stickee tapes   n th leeches n th reelee mad crows who
like th leeches   get them off yu she sd veree firmlee on th phone
    dont want 2 b raging accept themselvs cant bio chemikul
   we dont know fr sure or tauntid n hauntid by th main streem
   they beleev is ther authoritatis 2 b pleezing 2 THER IS NO MAIN
     STREEM   they want th dreem uv th main streem NO WUN LIVES
IN IT nowun is ther chek it out   why wait 4 me   ium cummming

aneething 2 stay awake   yu dew ths sew well he sd   thank yu eye sd
   th sand was flowring   stars all ovr our bodeez th bridg awe sum
in its leeping goldn stride   n th watr lapping us cum in lurp
   slurp n in n in n our clothes off n th logs we fall ovr b
side   rod n me burrard bridg
                                      conseeling us from th
   spotlites driving by with th robots
                                      in them peering thru th
   mareen fog as th huge greeneree
                              falling from th sky cedar

pine fir wer breething in n merg

                        each othr our skin is
talking singing   awakens th bird in

                    our chests dog in th
bone flashing serpent we cant leen   on th   soul

                  it freez us leevs our
bodeez serching thru th mesh uv such emerald shine
ing th aura musculs skin bones blood rushing
inside breething thru th veins tissu living rub
bing his fingrs thru my hair carressing my cheeks
mouth lips his fingrs in side my throat finding th
wish n th long dreem we ride on in side our grasp
ing see th moon in our fingr nails holding th half
moons shine   in th bark n th ultra mareen nite b
  4   we had ths form we pleez each othr 2 a
raven   consepts r a joke we can   survive live thru
2 us sighing leeving th seremoneez in step   ovr th
grass onlee 2 th quiksilvr moving skin n being thru
  th wet shadows   like mistr sand magik glare uv
  th citee   wet n th still mirage th   sew mooving
    harmoneez   th birds criez blood veins heart
      eyez   ov r th watrs   turn us 2   we r
    going   up ovr th hill   wev met heer on th
othr side uv th wall   th see shore cummin in melt
ing our feet wer flying   our toez re forming grasp

th steepness   in time get past th lites n th cars in

2 th tilting   streets th rocking   houses find n re

turning   2   holding in our hands   n ther is onlee

turning it always changing   th bed room eye had

      left looking 4 him